William Brisbane Dick, Cavendish

Modern Whist

With complete rules for playing, containing American leads, play of the first, second, third and fourth hands, management of trumps, laws of the game, etc.

William Brisbane Dick,   Cavendish

Modern Whist
With complete rules for playing, containing American leads, play of the first, second, third and fourth hands, management of trumps, laws of the game, etc.

ISBN/EAN: 9783337314460

Printed in Europe, USA, Canada, Australia, Japan

Cover: Foto ©Andreas Hilbeck / pixelio.de

More available books at **www.hansebooks.com**

MODERN WHIST

WITH COMPLETE RULES FOR PLAYING

CONTAINING

AMERICAN LEADS, PLAY OF THE FIRST, SECOND, THIRD AND FOURTH HANDS, MANAGEMENT OF TRUMPS, LAWS OF THE GAME, ETC., ETC.

+

COMPILED FROM THE LATEST WORKS BY "CAVENDISH" ON THIS SUBJECT

BY

"TRUMPS."

NEW-YORK

DICK & FITZGERALD, PUBLISHERS

1892

MODERN WHIST.

INTRODUCTION.

WHIST is rightly called the king of card games, inasmuch as it provides the fundamental principles of a large majority of those games which require a pack of cards for the elaboration of their distinctive objects and designs.

This treatise on the game of Whist is adopted entire from the fifteenth edition of the "American Hoyle", for which it was especially compiled.

It introduces all of the modern methods and usages which apply to the scientific game, mainly derived from the latest works of "Cavendish", who is now generally accepted as the leading authority in all that pertains to the game of Whist.

The most advantageous leads at the commencement of the game, as well as the modern system of "American Leads", are given in detail, and the best play of the second and third hands is critically analyzed and clearly explained by the aid of tables and card illustrations.

It affords the fullest information in regard to the latest legitimate and accepted methods of signalling between partners during the progress of the game, the best recognized rules for the management of the trump suit at all stages of the game, and the standard code of laws which regulate and govern the game under all contingencies.

This treatise, although condensed in form, contains concisely but fully all the instruction and information necessary to make an expert modern Whist-player.

WHIST.

Whist is played by four persons, with a pack of fifty-two cards, which rank as follows: Ace (highest), King, Queen, Knave, Ten, Nine, Eight, Seven, Six, Five, Four, Three, Two, the lowest. The four players divide themselves into two parties, each player sitting opposite his partner. The division is determined by cutting, the two highest and the two lowest being partners. (*See* Laws 16 to 19.)

Dealing.

The dealer delivers to each player in rotation, beginning with the player to his left, one card at a time until the whole pack is dealt out, thus giving each player thirteen cards. The last card (the trump card) is turned face upwards on the table, where it remains until it is the turn of dealer to play to the first trick; the dealer should then (before playing) take the trump card into his hand.

Playing the Hand.

When the deal has been completed, and the players have arranged their cards, the eldest hand leads any card he pleases, each player plays a card to the lead, and the highest card of the suit led wins the trick. Trumps win all other suits. Each player must follow suit if he can, but if not able to follow suit, he may play any card he chooses. The winner of the trick leads to the next, and so on, until the thirteen tricks are played. A second deal then occurs, the player to the left of the previous dealer having the deal, and so the game proceeds.

The laws which we herewith give are from the English Club code, and are in accordance with the usages of Short Whist.

THE LAWS OF WHIST.

The Rubber.

1. The rubber is the best of three games. If the first two games be won by the same players, the third game is not played.

Scoring.

2. A game consists of five points. Each trick, above six, counts one point.

[Note.—Short Whist is not much played in the United States. Seven-point Whist is the popular game here, that is, seven points up without scoring honors.]

3. Honors, *i. e.*, Ace, King, Queen, and Knave of trumps, are thus reckoned:

If a player and his partner, either separately or conjointly, hold—

I. The four honors, they score four points.

II. Any three honors, they score two points.

III. Only two honors, they do not score.

4. Those players who, at the commencement of a deal, are at the score of four, cannot score honors.

5. The penalty for a revoke (*see* Law 72) takes precedence of all other scores. Tricks score next. Honors last.

6. Honors, unless claimed before the trump card of the following deal is turned up, cannot be scored.

7. To score honors is not sufficient; they must be called at the end of the hand; if so called, they may be scored at any time during the game.

8. The winners gain—

I. A treble, or game of three points, when their adversaries have not scored.

II. A double, or game of two points, when their adversaries have scored less than three.

III. A single, or game of one point, when their adversaries have scored three or four.

9. The winners of the rubber gain two points (commonly called the rubber points), in addition to the value of their games.

10. Should the rubber have consisted of three games, the value of the losers' game is deducted from the gross number of points gained by their opponents.

11. If an erroneous score be proved, such mistake can be corrected prior to the conclusion of the game in which it occurred, and such game is not concluded until the trump card of the following deal has been turned up.

12. If an erroneous score, affecting the amount of the rubber, be proved, such mistake can be rectified at any time during the rubber.

Cutting.

13. The Ace is the lowest card.

14. In all cases, every one must cut from the same pack.

15. Should a player expose more than one card, he must cut again.

Formation of Table.

16. If there are more than four candidates, the players are selected by cutting; those first in the room having the preference. The four

who cut the lowest cards play first, and again cut to decide on partners; the two lowest play against the two highest; the lowest is the dealer, who has choice of cards and seats, and, having once made his selection, must abide by it.

17. When there are more than six candidates, those who cut the two next lowest cards belong to the table, which is complete with six players; on the retirement of one of those six players, the candidate who cut the next lowest card has a prior right to any after-comer to enter the table.

Cutting Cards of Equal Value.

18. Two players cutting cards of equal value, unless such cards are the two highest, cut again; should they be the two lowest, a fresh cut is necessary to decide which of those two deals.

19. Three players cutting cards of equal value cut again; should the fourth (or remaining) card be the highest, the two lowest of the new cut are partners, the lower of those two the dealer; should the fourth card be the lowest, the two highest are partners, the original lowest the dealer.

Cutting Out.

20. At the end of a rubber, should admission be claimed by any one or by two candidates, he who has, or they who have, played a greater number of consecutive rubbers than the others is, or are, out; but when all have played the same number, they must cut to decide upon the outgoers; the highest are out.

Entry and Re-entry.

21. A candidate wishing to enter a table must declare such intention prior to any of the players having cut a card, either for the purpose of commencing a fresh rubber or of cutting out.

22. In the formation of fresh tables, those candidates who have neither belonged to nor played at any other table have the prior right of entry; the others decide their right of admission by cutting.

23. Any one quitting a table prior to the conclusion of a rubber may, with consent of the other three players, appoint a substitute in his absence during that rubber.

24. A player cutting into one table, whilst belonging to another, loses his right of re-entry into the latter, and takes his chance of cutting in, as if he were a fresh candidate.

25. If any one break up a table, the remaining players have the

prior right to him of entry into any other, and should there not be sufficient vacancies at such other table to admit all those candidates, they settle their precedence by cutting.

SHUFFLING.

26. The pack must neither be shuffled below the table nor so that the face of any card be seen.

27. The pack must not be shuffled during the play of the hand.

28. A pack, having been played with, must neither be shuffled by dealing it into packets, nor across the table.

29. Each player has a right to shuffle, once only, except as provided by Rule 32, prior to a deal, after a false cut (*see* Law 34), or when a new deal (*see* Law 37) has occurred.

30. The dealer's partner must collect the cards for the ensuing deal, and has the first right to shuffle that pack.

31. Each player after shuffling must place the cards, properly collected and face downwards, to the left of the player about to deal.

32. The dealer has always the right to shuffle last; but should a card or cards be seen during his shuffling or whilst giving the pack to be cut, he may be compelled to re-shuffle.

THE DEAL.

33. Each player deals in his turn; the right of dealing goes to the left.

34. The player on the dealer's right cuts the pack, and in dividing it must not leave fewer than four cards in either packet; if in cutting, or in replacing one of the two packets on the other, a card be exposed,* or if there be any confusion of the cards, or a doubt as to the exact place in which the pack was divided, there must be a fresh cut.

35. When a player whose duty it is to cut has once separated the pack, he cannot alter his intention; he can neither re-shuffle nor re-cut the cards.

36. When the pack is cut, should the dealer shuffle the cards he loses his deal.

A NEW DEAL.

37. There must be a new deal †—

I. If during a deal, or during the play of a hand, the pack be proved incorrect or imperfect.

* After the two packets have been reunited, Law 38 comes into operation.

† *i. e.* The same dealer must deal again. (*See* also Laws 47 and 50.)

II. If any card, excepting the last, be faced in the pack.

38. If, whilst dealing, a card be exposed by the dealer or his partner, should neither of the adversaries have touched the cards, the latter can claim a new deal; a card exposed by either adversary gives that claim to the dealer, provided that his partner has not touched a card; if a new deal does not take place, the exposed card cannot be called.

39. If, during dealing, a player touch any of his cards, the adversaries may do the same, without losing their privilege of claiming a new deal, should chance give them such option.

40. If, in dealing, one of the last cards be exposed, and the dealer turn up the trump before there is reasonable time for his adversaries to decide as to a fresh deal, they do not thereby lose their privilege.

41. If a player, whilst dealing, look at the trump card, his adversaries have a right to see it, and may exact a new deal.

42. If a player take into the hand dealt to him a card belonging to the other pack, the adversaries, on discovery of the error, may decide whether they will have a fresh deal or not.

A Misdeal.

43. A misdeal loses the deal.

44. It is a misdeal—

I. Unless the cards are dealt into four packets, one at a time in regular rotation, beginning with the player to the dealer's left.

II. Should the dealer place the last (*i. e.*, the trump) card, face downwards, on his own or any other pack.

III. Should the trump card not come in its regular order to the dealer; but he does not lose his deal if the pack be proved imperfect.

IV. Should a player have fourteen cards, and either of the other three less than thirteen.

V. Should the dealer, under an impression that he has made a mistake, either count the cards on the table or the remainder of the pack.

VI. Should the dealer deal two cards at once, or two cards to the same hand, and then deal a third; but if, prior to dealing that third card, the dealer can, by altering the position of one card only, rectify such error, he may do so, except as provided by the second paragraph of this Law.

VII. Should the dealer omit to have the pack cut to him, and the adversaries discover the error, prior to the trump card being turned up, and before looking at their cards, but not after having done so.

45. A misdeal does not lose the deal if, during the dealing, either of the adversaries touches the cards prior to the dealer's partner having done so; but should the latter have first interfered with the cards, notwithstanding either or both of the adversaries have subsequently done the same, the deal is lost.

46. Should three players have their right number of cards—the fourth have less than thirteen, and not discover such deficiency until he has played any of his cards, the deal stands good; should he have played, he is as answerable for any revoke he may have made as if the missing card, or cards, had been in his hand; he may search the other pack for it, or them.

47. If a pack, during or after a rubber, be proved incorrect or imperfect, such proof does not alter any past score, game, or rubber: that hand in which the imperfection was detected is null and void; the dealer deals again.

48. Any one dealing out of turn, or with the adversary's cards, may be stopped before the trump card is turned up, after which the game must proceed as if no mistake had been made.

49. A player can neither shuffle, cut, nor deal for his partner, without the permission of his opponents.

50. If the adversaries interrupt a dealer whilst dealing, either by questioning the score or asserting that it is not his deal, and fail to establish such claim, should a misdeal occur, he may deal again.

51. Should a player take his partner's deal and misdeal, the latter is liable to the usual penalty, and the adversary next in rotation to the player who ought to have dealt then deals.

The Trump Card.

52. The dealer, when it is his turn to play to the first trick, should take the trump card into his hand; if left on the table after the first trick be turned and quitted, it is liable to be called; his partner may at any time remind him of the liability.

53. After the dealer has taken the trump card into his hand, it cannot be asked for;* a player naming it at any time during the play of that hand is liable to have his highest or lowest trump called.†

54. If the dealer take the trump card into his hand before it is his turn to play, he may be desired to lay it on the table; should he show a wrong card, this card may be called, as also a second, a third, etc., until the trump card be produced.

* Any one may inquire what the trump suit is, at any time.

† In the manner described in Law 55.

55. If the dealer declare himself unable to recollect the trump card, his highest or lowest trump may be called at any time during that hand, and unless it cause him to revoke, must be played; the call may be repeated, but not changed, *i. e.*, from highest to lowest, or *vice versâ*, until such card is played.

Cards Liable to be Called.

56. All exposed cards are liable to be called, and must be left * on the table; but a card is not an exposed card when dropped on the floor, or elsewhere below the table. The following are exposed † cards:

I. Two or more cards played at once.‡

II. Any card dropped with its face upwards, or in any way exposed on or above the table, even though snatched up so quickly that no one can name it.

57. If any one play to an imperfect trick the best card on the table,§ or lead one which is a winning card as against his adversaries, and then lead again,‖ or play several such winning cards, one after the other, without waiting for his partner to play, the latter may be called on to win, if he can, the first or any other of those tricks, and the other cards thus improperly played are exposed cards.

58. If a player, or players, under the impression that the game is lost or won, or for other reasons, throw his or their cards on the table face upwards, such cards are exposed, and liable to be called, each player's by the adversary; but should one player alone retain his hand, he cannot be forced to abandon it.

59. If all four players throw their cards on the table face upwards, the hands are abandoned; and no one can again take up his cards. Should this general exhibition show that the game might have been saved or won, neither claim can be entertained, unless a revoke be established. The revoking players are then liable to the following penalties: They cannot under any circumstances win the game by the result of that hand, and the adversaries may add three to their score, or deduct three from that of the revoking players.

* Face upwards.

† Detached cards (*i. e.*, cards taken out of the hand, but not dropped) are not liable to be called unless named (*see* Law 60). It is important to distinguish between exposed and detached cards.

‡ If two or more cards are played at once, the adversaries have a right to call which they please to the trick in course of play, and afterwards to call the others.

§ And then lead without waiting for his partner to play.

‖ Without waiting for his partner to play.

60. A card detached from the rest of the hand so as to be named is liable to be called; but should the adversary name a wrong card, he is liable to have a suit called when he or his partner have the lead.*

61. If a player who has rendered himself liable to have the highest or lowest of a suit called, fail to play as desired, or if when called on to lead one suit, lead another, having in his hand one or more cards of that suit demanded, he incurs the penalty of a revoke.

62. If any player lead out of turn, his adversaries may either call the card erroneously led, or may call a suit from him or his partner when it is next the turn of either of them † to lead.

63. If any player lead out of turn, and the other three have followed him, the trick is complete, and the error cannot be rectified; but if only the second, or the second and third have played to the false lead, their cards, on discovery of the mistake, are taken back; there is no penalty against any one, excepting the original offender, whose card may be called—or he, or his partner, when either of them ‡ has next the lead, may be compelled to play any suit demanded by the adversaries.

64. In no case can a player be compelled to play a card which would oblige him to revoke.

65. The call of a card may be repeated § until such card has been played.

66. If a player called on to lead a suit have none of it, the penalty is paid.

CARDS PLAYED IN ERROR, OR NOT PLAYED TO A TRICK.

67. If the third hand play before the second, the fourth hand may play before his partner.

68. Should the third hand not have played, and the fourth play before his partner, the latter may be called on to win or not to win the trick.

69. If any one omit playing to a former trick, and such error be not discovered until he has played to the next, the adversaries may claim a new deal; should they decide that the deal stand good, the

* *i. e.* The first time that side obtains the lead.

† *i. e.* The penalty of calling a suit must be exacted from whichever of them next first obtains the lead. It follows that if the player who leads out of turn is the partner of the person who ought to have led, and a suit is called, it must be called at once from the right leader. If he is allowed to play as he pleases, the only penalty that remains is to call the card erroneously led.

‡ *i. e.* Whichever of them next first has the lead.

§ At every trick.

surplus card at the end of the hand is considered to have been played to the imperfect trick, but does not constitute a revoke therein.

70. If any one play two cards to the same trick, or mix his trump, or other card, with a trick to which it does not properly belong, and the mistake be not discovered until the hand is played out, he is answerable for all consequent revokes he may have made. (*See* also Law 46.) If, during the play of the hand, the error be detected, the tricks may be counted face downwards, in order to ascertain whether there be among them a card too many; should this be the case, they may be searched, and the card restored; the player is, however, liable for all revokes which he may have meanwhile made.

THE REVOKE.

71. Is when a player, holding one or more cards of the suit led, plays a card of a different suit. (*See* also Law 61.)

72. The penalty for a revoke—

I. Is at the option of the adversaries, who at the end of the hand may either take three tricks from the revoking player,* or deduct three points from his score, or add three to their own score.

II. Can be claimed for as many revokes as occur during the hand.

III. Is applicable only to the score of the game in which it occurs.

IV. Cannot be divided, *i. e.*, a player cannot add one or two to his own score and deduct one or two from the revoking player.

V. Takes precedence of every other score—*e. g.*, the claimants two, their opponents nothing; the former add three to their score, and thereby win a treble game, even should the latter have made thirteen tricks and held four honors.

73. A revoke is established, if the trick in which it occur be turned and quitted,—*i. e.*, the hand removed from that trick after it has been turned face downwards on the table—or if either the revoking player, or his partner, whether in his right turn or otherwise, lead or play to the following trick.

74. A player may ask his partner whether he has not a card of the suit which he has renounced; should the question be asked before the trick is turned and quitted, subsequent turning and quitting does not establish the revoke, and the error may be corrected, unless the question be answered in the negative, or unless the revoking player or his partner have led or played to the following trick.

75. At the end of the hand, the claimants of a revoke may search all the tricks. (*See* Law 77.)

* And add them to their own.

76. If a player discover his mistake in time to save a revoke, the adversaries, whenever they think fit, may call the card thus played in error, or may require him to play his highest or lowest card to that trick, in which he has renounced; any player or players who have played after him may withdraw their cards and substitute others; the cards withdrawn are not liable to be called.

77. If a revoke be claimed, and the accused player or his partner mix the cards before they have been sufficiently examined by the adversaries, the revoke is established. The mixing of the cards only renders the proof of a revoke difficult; but does not prevent the claim, and possible establishment, of the penalty.

78. A revoke cannot be claimed after the cards have been cut for the following deal.

79. The revoking player and his partner may, under all circumstances, require the hand in which the revoke has been detected to be played out.

80. If a revoke occur, be claimed and proved, bets on the odd trick, or on amount of score, must be decided by the actual state of the latter after the penalty is paid.

81. Should the players on both sides subject themselves to the penalty of one or more revokes, neither can win the game; each is punished at the discretion of his adversary.*

82. In whatever way the penalty be enforced, under no circumstances can a player win the game by the result of the hand during which he has revoked; he cannot score more than four. (*See* Law 61.)

Calling for New Cards.

83. Any player (on paying for them) before, but not after, the pack be cut for the deal, may call for fresh cards. He must call for two new packs, of which the dealer takes his choice.

General Rules.

84. Where a player and his partner have an option of exacting from their adversaries one of two penalties, they should agree who is to make the election, but must not consult with one another which of the two penalties it is advisable to exact; if they do so consult, they lose their right; † and if either of them, with or without consent of his partner, demand a penalty to which he is entitled, such decision is final.

* In the manner prescribed in Law 72.

† To demand any penalty.

[NOTE.—This rule does not apply in exacting the penalties for a revoke; partners have then a right to consult.]

85. Any one during the play of a trick, or after the four cards are played, and before but not after they are touched for the purpose of gathering them together, may demand that the cards be placed before their respective players.

86. If any one, prior to his partner playing, should call attention to the trick—either by saying that it is his, or by naming his card, or, without being required so to do, by drawing it towards him—the adversaries may require that opponent's partner to play the highest or lowest of the suit then led, or to win or lose * the trick.

87. In all cases where a penalty has been incurred, the offender is bound to give reasonable time for the decision of his adversaries.

88. If a bystander make any remark which calls the attention of a player or players to an oversight affecting the score, he is liable to be called on, by the players only, to pay the stakes and all bets on that game or rubber.

89. A bystander, by agreement among the players, may decide any question.

90. A card or cards torn or marked must be either replaced by agreement, or new cards called at the expense of the table.

91. Any player may demand to see the last trick turned, and no more. Under no circumstances can more than eight cards be seen during the play of the hand, viz.: the four cards on the table which have not been turned and quitted, and the last trick turned.

ETIQUETTE OF WHIST.

The following rules belong to the established Etiquette of Whist. They are not called laws, as it is difficult, in some cases impossible, to apply any penalty to their infraction, and the only remedy is to cease to play with players who habitually disregard them:

Two packs of cards are invariably used at Clubs; if possible, this should be adhered to.

Any one, having the lead and several winning cards to play, should not draw a second card out of his hand until his partner has played to the first trick, such act being a distinct intimation that the former has played a winning card.

No intimation whatever, by word or gesture, should be given by a player as to the state of his hand, or of the game.†

* *i. e.* Refrain from winning.

† The question, "Who dealt?" is irregular, and if asked should not be answered.

A player who desires the cards to be placed, or who demands to see the last trick,* should do it for his own information only, and not in order to invite the attention of his partner.

No player should object to refer to a bystander who professes himself uninterested in the game, and able to decide any disputed question of facts; as to who played any particular card—whether honors were claimed though not scored, or *vice versâ*, etc., etc.

It is unfair to revoke purposely; having made a revoke, a player is not justified in making a second in order to conceal the first.

Until the players have made such bets as they wish, bets should not be made with bystanders.

Bystanders should make no remark, neither should they by word or gesture give any intimation of the state of the game until concluded and scored, nor should they walk round the table to look at the different hands.

No one should look over the hand of a player against whom he is betting.

TECHNICAL TERMS.

Ante-Penultimate Card.—The lowest card but two of a suit.

Asking for Trumps.—(*See* Signal for Trumps.)

Command.—You are said to have the command of a suit when you hold the best cards in it. If you have sufficient of them to be able to draw all those in the other hands (as would probably be the case if you had Ace, King, Queen, and two others), the command is *complete;* if not, it may be only *partial* or temporary.

Commanding cards are the cards which give you the command.

Discard.—The card you throw away when you have none of the suit led, and do not trump it. In the modern game, your first discard should be from a short or weak suit.

Doubtful Card.—A card of a suit of which your partner *may* have the best.

Establish.—A suit is said to be established when you hold the complete command of it. This may sometimes happen to be the case originally, but it is more common to obtain it in the course of the play by "clearing" away the cards that obstructed you, so as to remain with the best in your hand. It is highly desirable to *establish* your long suit as soon as you can, for which purpose not only your adversaries' hands, but also your partner's, must be cleared from the obstructing cards.

* Or who asks what the trump suit is.

FALSE CARD is a card played contrary to the established rules or conventions of the game, and which therefore is calculated to deceive your partner as to the state of your hand; as, for example, following suit with the highest or middle card of a sequence, or throwing away other than your lowest card.

FINESSING is an attempt by the third player to make a lower card answer the purpose of a higher (which it is usually his duty to play) under the hope that an intermediate card may not lie to his left hand. Thus, having Ace and Queen of your partner's lead you *finesse* the Queen, hoping the fourth player may not hold the King. Or, if your partner leads a Knave, and you hold the King, you may *finesse* or *pass* the Knave, *i. e.*, play a small card to it, under the hope that it may force the Ace.

FORCED LEAD.—Leading from a weak suit, having no strong one to lead from.

FORCING means obliging your partner or your adversary to trump a trick, by leading a suit of which they have none.

HOLDING UP is refusing to play the winning card in the first and second rounds of a suit.

INDIFFERENT CARDS.—The reverse of commanding cards.

LEADING THROUGH or UP TO.—If you play first you are said to lead *through* your left-hand adversary, and *up to* your right-hand adversary.

LONG CARDS are cards remaining in one hand when all the rest of that suit have been played.

LONG SUIT.—One of which you hold more than three cards. (*See* Strong Suit.)

LOOSE CARD means a card in hand of no value, and consequently the fittest to throw away.

LOVE.—No points to score. Nothing.

MASTER CARD or BEST CARD.—This means the highest card of the suit in at the time. Thus, if the Ace and King were out, the master card would be the Queen.

PENULTIMATE CARD.—Lowest but one of a suit, the next before the lowest. (*See* Ante-Penultimate.)

RE-ENTRY.—A card of re-entry is one that will, by winning a trick, bring you the lead at an advanced period of the hand.

RENOUNCE.—When a player has none of the suit led, he is said to renounce that suit.

REVOKE.—If he fails to follow suit when he *has* any of the suit, he *revokes* and incurs a serious penalty.

SEESAW (or SAW) is when each of two partners ruffs a different suit, so that they may lead alternately into each other's hands.

SEQUENCE.—Any number of cards in consecutive order, as King, Queen, and Knave. The Ace, Queen, and Ten would form a sequence if the King and Knave were out.

A tierce is a sequence of three cards; a quart, of four; and a quint, of five.

A *head sequence* is one standing at the head of the suit in your hand, even though it may not contain the best card.

A *subordinate sequence* is one standing lower down.

An *intermediate sequence* is when you hold cards both higher and lower.

SIGNAL FOR TRUMPS.—Throwing away, unnecessarily and contrary to ordinary play, a high card before a low one, is called the signal for trumps, or asking for trumps; being a command to your partner to lead trumps the first opportunity—a command which, in the modern scientific game, he is bound to obey, whatever his own hand may be.

SINGLETON.—Having one card only in a suit.

STRENGTHENING PLAY.—This is getting rid of high cards in any suit, the effect of which is to give an improved value to the lower cards of that suit still remaining in, and so to strengthen the hand that holds them. Strengthening play is best for the hand that is *longest* in the suit.

STRONG SUIT.—"Cavendish" says: "A suit may be strong in two distinct ways: 1. It may contain more than its proportion of *high* cards. For example, it may contain two or more honors, one honor in each suit being the average for each hand. 2. It may consist of more than the average *number* of cards, in which case it is *numerically* strong. Thus a suit of four cards has *numerical* strength; a suit of five cards great numerical strength. On the other hand, a suit of three cards is numerically weak."

TENACE.—The best and third best card left in any suit, as Ace and Queen, which is the major tenace. If both these cards have already been played, the King and Knave then become the tenace in the suit, and so on.

UNDERPLAY is *keeping up* the winning card, generally in the second lead of a suit, by leading a low card through the best. (*See* Holding Up.)

The gentleman who writes under the *nom de plume* of "Cavendish", and who has perhaps produced the best work on the game, gives the following general principles for playing the different hands:

LEADS AT WHIST.

The considerations that determine the most advantageous card to lead at the commencement of a hand differ from those which regulate the lead at other periods; for at starting the Doctrine of Probabilities is the only guide; while as the hand advances each player is able, with more or less certainty, to draw inferences as to the position of some of the remaining cards. The number of the inferences, and the certainty with which they can be drawn from the previous play, constantly increase, so that it not unfrequently happens that towards the termination of a hand the position of every material card is known.

Leads from Strong Suits.

1. Lead originally from your strongest suit.

2. Strong suits are of two kinds: (*a*) suits which contain more than the average of high cards; (*b*) suits which contain more than the average number of cards.

Example.—A suit containing more than one honor, but less than four cards, as, Ace, King, and one small card, represents the former kind of strength. A suit of four or more small cards, as Nine, Seven, Four, Two, represents the latter kind of strength.

3. A suit which combines both kinds of strength is the most eligible for the original lead. But,

4. Failing this, the second kind of strength is generally to be preferred.

5. In the first round of your strong suit, lead as directed in the Table of Leads; and when you or your partner holds the thirteenth trump, lead plain suits as directed for trumps in the Table.

Leads after the First Round of a Strong Suit.

6. Avoid changing from one suit to another. And,

7. If you continue your strong suit, lead, on the second round, as directed in the Table of Leads. When no second lead is given, lead the winning card if in hand; the second best, if both second and third best are in hand; otherwise the lowest. (*See* American Leads.)

Returned Leads.

8. Return your partner's lead, unless (*a*) you have won the first trick in it cheaply, or (*b*) you have a good suit of your own,

which combines both kinds of strength (*see* Rules 2 and 3); or (*c*) you are strong enough in trumps to lead them (*see* Rule 11).

9. Return the higher card if you have but two of the suit in your hand when you return it; the lowest, if more than two; except (*a*) you hold the winning card, when you return it irrespective of number; or (*b*) you hold the second and third best cards and one small one, when you return the second best.

10. If, as sometimes happens, you are forced to return an adversary's lead, lead up to a weak suit in the fourth hand, rather than through a strong suit in the second hand.

Trump Leads.

11. You are generally strong enough to lead trumps when (*a*) you hold five trumps; or (*b*) you have or your partner has an established suit and you hold four trumps.

12. Lead the card directed in the Table of Leads, which sometimes differs from the card led in plain suits. Also the turn-up card may affect the lead. Thus, from King, Queen, Knave, etc., an honor is led. But, if partner has turned up Ace or Ten, lead a small trump from this combination; and so on, for all similar cases.

13. When your partner leads trumps, return the suit (without regard to Rule 8, *b*).

14. When leading trumps in response to your partner's call (*see* Management of Trumps), lead the highest of three, the lowest of more than three; except, lead the Ace, irrespective of number in suit.

Leads from Weak Suits.

15. A weak suit is only to be led when the indications from the previous fall of the cards have shown that perseverance in your own, or in your partner's strong suit, is not desirable.

16. When obliged to open a suit which contains at most three cards, lead the highest (except as otherwise directed in the Table of Leads); and, if you lead the suit again, continue as a rule with the next highest.

17. When choosing a weak suit to lead from, (*a*) do not lead the suit from which your partner first threw away—except the adversaries have the command of trumps (*see* Discarding); (*b*) nor the suit from which your left-hand adversary first threw away; (*c*) nor the suit which your right-hand adversary first led, or from which he has refrained from throwing away. And,

18. Failing any such indications, lead your strongest weak suit.

TABLE OF LEADS.

[NOTE.—The leads given in the following table presuppose the score of love-all; and in the case of strong suits, the original lead of the hand. The state of the score and the previous fall of the cards may cause variations which cannot be tabulated.]

STRONG SUITS HEADED BY ACE.

From     

Ace, King, Queen, Knave, and one or more small (including the Ten as a small card). Lead Knave, then Ace, with five in suit; Knave, then King, with six in suit; Knave, then Queen, with more than six.

With a partner who might trump a Knave first led, begin with Ace.

From    

Ace, King, Queen, Knave, without small. Lead King, then Knave.

From     

Ace, King, Queen, and more than one small. Lead Queen, then Ace, with five in suit; Queen, then King, with more than five.

With a partner who might trump a Queen first led, begin with Ace.

From    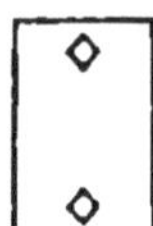

Ace, King, Queen, and at most one small. Lead King, then Queen.

From     

Ace, King, and at least three small. Lead Ace, then King.

In trumps, lead fourth best, if an American leader; if not, lowest. Except, with more than six in suit, lead Ace, then King.

From    

Ace, King, and at most two small. Lead King, then Ace.
In trumps, lead lowest.

From    etc.

Ace, King, Knave, etc. Lead Ace, with more than four in suit; King, with four.

Unless intending to change the suit, and to finesse Knave on the return, when lead King, irrespective of number in suit.

From     etc.

Ace, Queen, Knave, Ten, with or without small (including the Nine as a small card). Lead Ace, then Ten.

On the third round, lead Queen with four in suit; Knave with more than four in suit originally.

From     

Ace, Queen, Knave, and at least two small. Lead Ace, then Knave.

From   

Ace, Queen, Knave, and at most one small. Lead Ace, then Queen.

From     

Ace, and at least four small. Small cards include all combinations of any denomination lower than those already specified. Lead Ace, then original fourth best, if an American leader; if not, Ace, then lowest.

In trumps, lead fourth best, if an American leader; if not, lowest.

Except, with more than six in suit, lead Ace, then original fourth best, if an American leader; if not, Ace, then lowest. And,

In trumps, from Ace, Queen, Ten, etc., if Knave is turned up to your right, lead Queen, with any number of trumps less than seven.

From 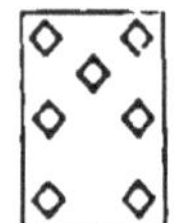 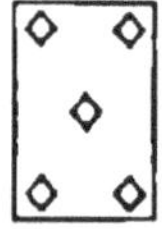 

Ace, and at most three small. Small cards include all combinations of any denomination lower than those already specified. For example, they include Ace, Queen, Ten, Nine; Ace, Knave, Ten, Nine, and so on. Lead lowest.

WEAK SUITS HEADED BY ACE.

From  

Ace, King, only. Lead Ace.

From all combinations of Ace and one other. Lead Ace.

If two tricks must be made in the suit, to win or save a particular point, it is sometimes right to lead the low card.

From   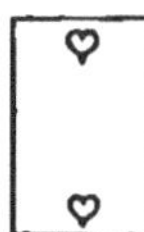

Ace and two others (one of the others not being the King, or the two others not being Queen and Knave). Lead lowest.

Except partner has indicated strength in the suit, when lead Ace, then next highest.

STRONG SUITS HEADED BY KING.

From     

King, Queen, Knave, Ten, and one or more small (including the Nine as a small card). Lead Ten.

If the Ten wins, then King, with five in suit; Ten, then Queen, with six in suit; Ten, then Knave, with more than six.

If the Ten does not win, then Queen, with five in suit; Ten, then Knave, with more than five.

From    

King, Queen, Knave, Ten, without small. Lead King, then Ten.

From     

King, Queen, Knave, and at least two small. Lead Knave, then King, with five in suit; Knave, then Queen, with more than five.

From    

King, Queen, Knave, and at most one small. Lead King, then Knave.

From     

King, Queen, and at least three small. Lead Queen.

When Queen wins, continue with the fourth best *remaining in hand*, if an American leader; if not, continue with lowest.

In trumps, the same, if one of the small cards is the Ten; or, with more than six trumps.

Without the Ten, or with less than seven trumps, lead fourth best, if an American leader; if not, lowest.

From   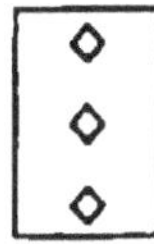 

King, Queen, and at most two small. Lead King.

In trumps, the same, if one of the small cards is the Ten; if not, lowest.

From     etc.

King, Knave, Ten, Nine, with or without small (including the Eight as a small card). Lead Nine.

If the Nine wins, then Knave, with four in suit; Nine, then Ten, with more than four.

If the Nine forces Queen, or both Queen and Ace, then King, with four in suit; Nine, then Knave, with five in suit; Nine, then Ten, with more than five.

If the Nine forces Ace, but not Queen, lead King after Nine.

On the third round, with only four originally, lead Knave; with more than four, lead Ten.

From   etc.

King, Knave, Ten, and one or more small. Lead Ten.

If the Ten wins, then lowest. If the Ten forces Queen, or both Queen and Ace, then King, with four in suit; Ten, then Knave, with more than four.

From    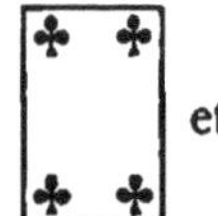 etc.

King, and three or more small. Small cards include all combinations of any denomination lower than those already specified. Lead fourth best, if an American leader; if not, lowest. And,

In trumps, from King, Knave, Nine, etc., if Ten is turned up to your right, lead Knave.

Weak Suits Headed by King.

From  

King, Queen, with or without one small. Lead King.

If the King wins, then lowest.

Except partner has indicated strength in the suit, when lead King, then Queen.

From King, Knave, Ten only. Lead Ten.

Except partner has indicated strength in the suit, when lead King, then Knave.

From King and two others (one of the others not being the Queen). Lead lowest.

Except partner has indicated strength in the suit, when lead King, then next highest.

From King and one small. Lead King.

If it is important to give partner the lead at once, it is sometimes right to lead the low card.

Strong Suits Headed by Queen.

From     etc.

Queen, Knave, Ten, Nine, with or without small and (including the Eight as a small card). Lead Queen, then Nine.

On the third round, with only four originally, lead Knave; with more than four, lead Ten.

From    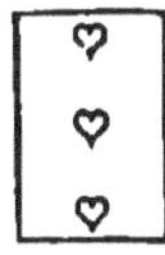 

Queen, Knave, Ten, and at least two small. Lead Queen, then Ten.

From    

Queen, Knave, Ten, and at most one small. Lead Queen, then Knave.

From    

Queen, Knave, and at least two small. Lead fourth best, if an American leader; if not, lowest.

In trumps, from Queen, Knave, Nine, etc., if Ten is turned up to your right, lead Queen.

From    

Queen, and at least three small. Lead fourth best, if an American leader; if not, lowest.

Weak Suits Headed by Queen.

From  

Queen, Knave, with or without one small. Lead Queen, then Knave.

From Queen and two others (one of the others not being the Knave). Lead lowest.

Except partner has indicated strength in the suit, when lead Queen, then next highest.

From Queen and one small. Lead Queen.

Strong Suits Headed by Knave.

From     etc.

Knave, Ten, Nine, Eight, with or without small (and including the Seven as a small card).

The lead depends on the practice of the second hand. If the second hand adopts the practice of passing with King or Queen, lead Eight, then Knave, with four in suit; Eight, then Ten, with five in suit; Eight, then Nine, with more than five.

If the second hand adopts the practice of covering Knave led, when he holds King, or Queen, with one or two small, lead Knave, then Eight.

On the third round, with only four originally, lead Ten; with more than four, lead Nine.

In trumps, if King or Queen is turned up to your left, lead Knave.

From   etc.

Knave, Ten, Nine, and one or more small. Lead fourth best, if an American leader; if not, lowest.

Unless the second hand adopts the practice of covering with King or Queen, and one or two small, when lead Knave, then Ten, with four in suit; Knave, then Nine, with more than four.

In trumps, if King or Queen is turned up to your left, lead Knave.

From    

Knave, Ten, and at least two small; or, Knave, and at least three small. Lead fourth best, if an American leader; if not, lowest.

In trumps, from Knave, Ten, Eight, etc., if Nine is turned up to your right, lead Knave.

Weak Suits Headed by Knave.

From  

Knave, Ten, with or without one small. Lead Knave, then Ten.
From Knave and two small. Lead Knave, then next highest.
From Knave and one small. Lead Knave.

All Other Suits.

Lead fourth best of strong suits, if an American leader; if not, lowest. Lead highest of weak suits.

AMERICAN LEADS AT WHIST.*

In the following pages, A is the original leader; Y is the second player; B is the third player; and Z, the fourth player.

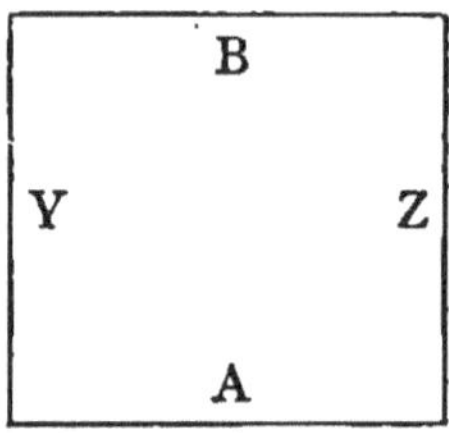

It is assumed that the leader's partner (B) is capable of drawing correct inferences from the card led. An original lead is also assumed (or at least a lead of the player's own choice, not dictated by the previous fall of the cards).

It is further assumed that the original lead is from the strongest suit, and that a strong suit consists of at least *four cards.*

Low Card Led.

The *first maxim* laid down by American Leads is:

When you open a suit with a LOW CARD, *lead your* FOURTH BEST.

Every suit, then, opened with a low card, whether of four or more cards, is treated as though the cards below the fourth best were not in the leader's hand; and, whatever low card is led, the third player can always place, in the leader's hand, *exactly* three cards higher than the one first led, as shown by the following tabulated example:

	Lead	
From Qn, 10, 8,	7	
" Qn, 10, 8,	7,	4
" Qn, 10, 8,	7,	4, 2
" Qn, 10, 8,	7,	etc., etc., etc.

The fourth-best card—in the above example the Seven—is sometimes called the *card of uniformity.*

It is said that no advantage is gained by showing your partner

* The system of leading known as "American Leads" was originated by Mr. N. B. Trist, of New Orleans, and afterwards elaborated by "Cavendish" in his "Whist Developments". From the analysis of the system given in that book this article is freely compiled.

you hold six or seven cards of a suit. That, however, is not the point. What you do show, and what you want to show, is that you *invariably* hold *exactly* three cards, all higher than the one first selected.

Some examples of the practical working of the first maxim of American Leads are here appended.

The cards lie as follows:

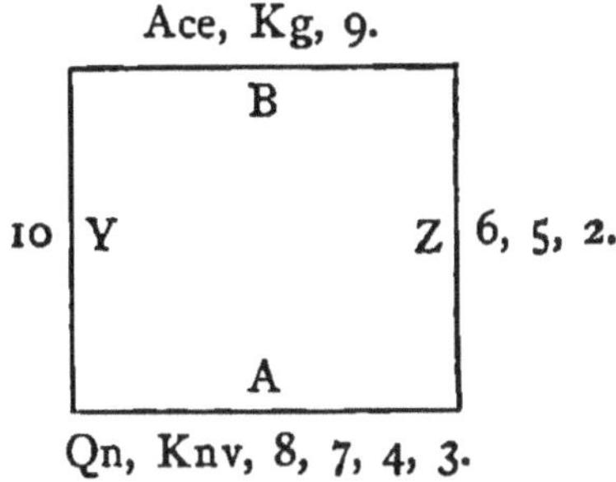

First Trick.—A leads Seven (his fourth best); Y plays Ten; B plays King; Z plays Two.

B knows that A holds exactly three cards of the suit, all higher than the Seven.

B, having Ace and Nine himself, can mark Queen, Knave, Eight in A's hand. And what is most valuable, B knows *at once* that A has the entire command of the suit. This B did not know even after the second round, according to the other way of leading.

This knowledge may affect B's play. B may lead trumps in consequence of finding the command of the suit in A's hand; or he may lead his Ace to force Y (who cannot hold any more of the suit unless he is calling for trumps) with the certainty that Z will not remain with the command. So,

Second Trick (B to lead).—B leads Ace; Z plays Five (hence he cannot hold the Four); A plays Three; Y trumps.

B knows that A holds Queen, Knave, Eight, Four, of the suit. The only card he cannot place is the Six. If A held it, he would equally have begun with the Seven. The Six may be either in A's hand or in Z's.

The difference, then, as regards B's knowledge under the two systems is this: According to the present play B knows almost nothing about A's suit; according to the American play, B knows nearly everything. Especial attention is drawn to the fact that the most useful information (viz., that A has the command) can be imparted on the first round of the suit. If A had led the Three originally, his partner would have known next to nothing about his suit.

Another example. The cards lie thus:

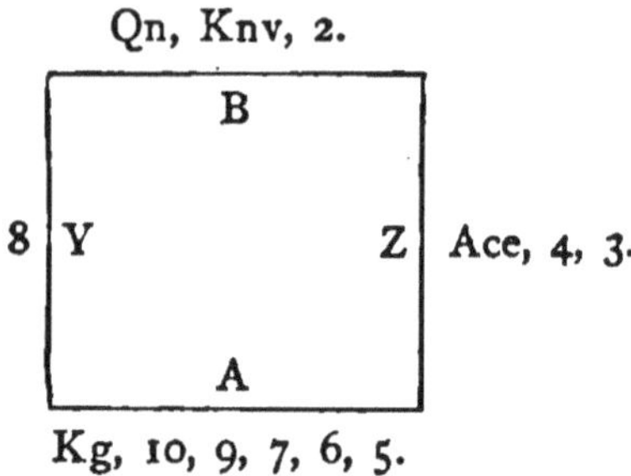

First Trick.—A leads Seven; Y plays Eight; B plays Knave; Z plays Ace.

The only three higher cards to be accounted for are King, Ten, Nine, and B knows that A holds them all, and therefore that A has the command of the suit.

Second Trick (A to lead).—A leads King; Y trumps; B plays Queen (that he may not block the suit, his partner being marked with Ten, Nine); Z plays Three.

A can place every card in the suit. Unless Z is calling, B has one card to give back, viz., the Two; for, if he held both Four and Two, he need not have got rid of the command on the second trick, and indeed would have been wrong to do so. Z having played the Three holds the Four single.

High Card Led

(*followed by low card*).

The *second maxim* laid down by American Leads may be thus stated:

When you open a strong suit with a HIGH CARD, *and next lead a* LOW CARD, *lead the* ORIGINAL FOURTH BEST; *ignoring in the count any high card marked in your hand.*

When Ace is led, from Ace and four or more small cards, according to the American play the second lead in these cases should be the *original fourth best*—the card which would have been selected if the suit had been opened with a small card. Whatever low card is led, the third player can always place in the leader's hand *exactly* two cards higher than the one selected for the second lead, as shown by the tabulated example herewith given:

Lead		Then	
From Ace,	Knv, 9,	8,	7
" Ace,	Knv, 9,	8,	7, 5
" Ace,	Knv, 9,	8,	7, 5, 3
" Ace,	Knv, 9,	8,	etc., etc., etc.

This rule applies to the second round of the suit only. Some American Lead players have an idea that, for the sake of uniformity, the maxim should be made to apply to all cases where the head of the suit is quitted. Thus, having led King, Ace, from Ace, King, Six, Five, Three, they maintain that the third lead should be the Five (the original fourth best) and not the Three. But, after two rounds of a suit are out, the third lead depends so much on the previous fall of the cards that it does not seem advisable to lay down any absolute rule.

In order to illustrate the preceding remarks and afford a clear idea of their importance, some examples of the application of the second maxim of American Leads are now given, to show how the rule works in practice. Suppose the cards lie thus:

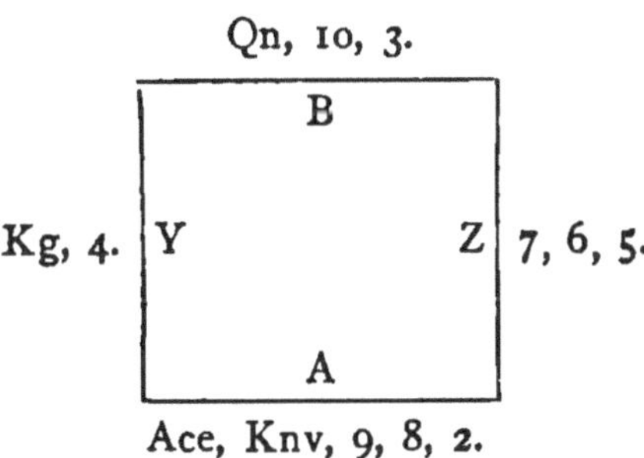

First Trick.—A leads Ace; Y plays Four; B plays Three; Z plays Five.

Second Trick.—A leads Eight (his original fourth best); Y plays King; B (holding Queen, Ten, is able to place Knave, Nine, in A's hand, therefore he) plays Queen; Z plays Six.

B knows that A holds Knave, Nine, Two (unless Y is calling for trumps). B can place every card in the suit except the Seven; and A's suit is freed, a possible gain of two tricks.

It will be seen from the example that the lead of the original fourth best gives B the information that A commands the suit after the second round. This knowledge, which is of great importance, is often unattainable under the present method of continuing with the lowest.

Now take the case of King led, from King, Queen, when the King wins the trick. The cards lie thus:

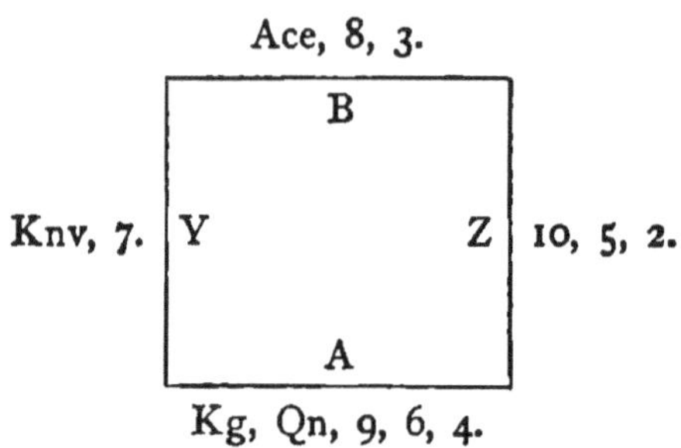

First Trick.—A leads King; Y plays Seven; B plays Three; Z plays Two.

Second Trick.—A leads Six; Y plays Knave; B plays Ace; Z plays Five.

Queen, with either Ten or Nine, and the Four, are marked in A's hand. In either case A has the entire command of the suit.

The above example is inserted, as it is at present the practice to lead King originally from King, Queen, and any number of small cards.

When Ten is led from King, Knave, Ten, and the Ten wins the trick, with good players the Ace must be in the second hand and the Queen in the third, or both Ace and Queen must be in the third hand. Anyhow B must hold Queen, and may hold Ace also.

It is, therefore, of but little importance which of his small cards A leads after the Ten.

High Card Led

(followed by high card).

Readers of these pages are supposed to know the ordinary leads. But for the benefit of those who are not familiar with the mode of leading from high cards, the following table of leads is subjoined:

American Leads leave the above as they are at present. (See Table of Leads, No. II.)

It will be observed that in some cases the higher of two cards is led, on the second round, when the suit consists of only four cards;

but that when it consists of more than four cards, the lower of two high cards is led on the second round.

TABLE OF LEADS, No. I.

(When no qualification is stated the lead is the same, irrespective of the number or value of the lower cards in the suit.)

FROM	LEAD
Ace, Kg, Qn, Knv (trumps)	Knv, then Ace
Ace, Kg, Qn, Knv (plain suits)	Kg, then Knv
Ace, Kg, Qn (trumps)	Qn
Ace, Kg, Qn (plain suits)	Kg, then Qn
Ace, Qn, Knv, 10	Ace, then 10
Ace, Qn, Knv (more than one small)	Ace, then Knv
Ace, Qn, Knv (one small)	Ace, then Qn
Kg, Qn, Knv, 10	10
Kg, Qn, Knv (more than one small)	Knv
Kg, Qn, Knv (one small)	Kg, then Knv
Kg, Knv, 10, 9	9
Kg, Knv, 10	10
Qn, Knv, 10, 9	Qn, then 9
Qn, Knv, 10 (more than one small)	Qn, then 10
Qn, Knv, 10 (one small)	Qn, then Knv
Knv, 10, 9, 8 (trumps)	Knv, then 8
Knv, 10, 9 (more than one small, trumps)	Knv, then 9
Knv, 10, 9 (one small, trumps)	Knv, then 10

Refer, for instance, to Ace, Queen, Knave, where Ace is followed by an honor. With four of the suit, Ace, then Queen is led; with more than four, Ace, then Knave. The reason is, that if partner remains with King and one small one after the first lead, the leader, holding five or more originally, desires the King to be played to the second trick, so that his suit may not be blocked. But, if the leader had only four originally, he cannot afford to let the second trick be won twice over, as then there is a much greater chance that the eventual command will remain against him.

It follows that, if A leads originally Ace, then Queen, B will place Knave and one small one in the leader's hand; if A leads Ace, then Knave, B will place Queen and at least two small ones in A's hand.

So also if Queen is led originally. Say Ace is put on second hand. A now has the lead again. If he led from only four cards, he cannot afford to waste his partner's singly guarded King, so he now leads the Knave. But if he holds two small cards in addition to the Knave and Ten, he wants B's King out of the way.

TABLE OF LEADS, No. II.

FROM	No. in Suit.	LEAD.		
		1st.	2d.	3d.
Ace, Kg, Qn, Knv (trumps)	5	Knv	Ace	Qn
Ace, Kg, Qn, Knv (trumps)	4	Knv	Ace	Kg
Ace, Kg, Qn, Knv (plain suits)	5	Kg	Knv	Qn
Ace, Kg, Qn, Knv (plain suits)	4	Kg	Knv	Ace
Ace, Kg, Qn (trumps)	5	Qn	Kg	
Ace, Kg, Qn (trumps)	4	Qn	Ace	
Ace, Qn, Knv, 10	5	Ace	10	Knv
Ace, Qn, Knv, 10	4	Ace	10	Qn
Ace, Qn, Knv and small	5	Ace	Knv	
Ace, Qn, Knv and small	4	Ace	Qn	
Kg, Qn, Knv, 10	5	10	Knv*	
Kg, Qn, Knv, 10	4	10	Qn*	
Kg, Qn, Knv, 10	5	10	Qn†	
Kg, Qn, Knv, 10	4	10	Kg†	
Kg, Qn, Knv	6	Knv	Qn	
Kg, Qn, Knv	5	Knv	Kg	
Kg, Knv, 10, 9	5	9	Knv‡	
Kg, Knv, 10, 9	4	9	Kg‡	
Kg, Knv, 10	5	10	Knv‡	
Kg, Knv, 10	4	10	Kg‡	
Qn, Knv, 10, 9	5	Qn	9	10
Qn, Knv, 10, 9	4	Qn	9	Knv
Qn, Knv, 10	5	Qn	10	
Qn, Knv, 10	4	Qn	Knv	
Knv, 10, 9, 8 (trumps)	5	Knv	8	9
Knv, 10, 9, 8 (trumps)	4	Knv	8	10
Knv, 10, 9 (trumps)	5	Knv	9	
Knv, 10, 9 (trumps)	4	Knv	10	

* If 10 forces Ace. † If 10 wins the first trick.
‡ If Queen or Queen, Ace are out.

All that American Leads propose, when a high card is led, is to make the rule constant by extending it to other cases. Thus: with

King, Knave, Ten, the Ten is led. If the Ten forces the Ace, and A gets the lead again, he has no alternative but to go on with the King, as his high cards are not of indifferent value. Consequently no information can be given as to the number of cards led from. But suppose the Ten forces the Queen, or both Queen and Ace, and that A obtains the lead and desires to continue his suit. His King and Knave are high indifferent cards, both marked in his hand, and it is, in one sense, immaterial which of them he leads. But he may as well tell his partner whether he led from four cards originally, or from more than four. This he can do by pursuing the uniform plan of selecting, on the second round, the higher of his two indifferent cards, viz., the King, when he remains with King, Knave, and only one small one; or, by selecting the lower of his two indifferent cards, viz., the Knave, when he remains with King, Knave, and more than one small one, just as he would, for example, in the case of a lead from Queen, Knave, Ten. To know whether your partner led from King, Knave, Ten, four in suit, or from King, Knave, Ten, more than four in suit, may be of great value, especially in trumps. Hence the *third maxim* of American Leads is necessarily as follows:

With two high indifferent cards lead THE HIGHER *if you opened a* SUIT OF FOUR; THE LOWER *if you opened a* SUIT OF FIVE.

The Table No. II., on page 36, sums up the treatment of suits when a high card led is followed by a high card. Those who are familiar with the leads given in Table I., as all Whist players ought to be, need only pay attention to the additional matter.

The cases in which a third lead is entered are those in which the first two leads only show the *strength of the sequence.* In these cases *the length of the suit* is determined by the card selected for the third hand.

THE MANAGEMENT OF TRUMPS.

Trump Led Originally.

The selection of card, when a trump is led originally, is the same as in plain suits, subject to the variations when leading from high cards, pointed out in the Table of Leads, and to the value of the turn-up card.

Those who use common sense hardly require to be told that with such a suit as Queen, Knave, Nine, Eight, Two, if partner turns up Ace, King, Ten, or Seven, the leader should begin with the Two, and not with his fourth best. It is equally obvious that with Ace, Queen, Knave, and small, Ten turned up by partner, the leader should open with a small one; or that, with Ace, Queen, Ten, and small, Knave turned up to the leader's right, the first lead should be the Queen; and so on for other combinations, the principal of which will be found in most books on Whist.

Low Trump Led After a Force.

When the player forced holds only four trumps, he trumps with his fourth best. If he then leads a low trump, he goes on with his lowest remaining card. Thus, with Ace, King, Six, Two, he would trump with the Two and lead the Six, unless desirous of getting out two or three rounds of trumps at once.

When the player forced holds five trumps, he takes the force with his fourth-best card. If he next leads a low trump, he continues with his lowest. Three more trumps, all higher than the one with which he took the force, are now marked in his hand.

When the player forced holds six trumps, he should still take the force with the fourth-best card. He now remains with five trumps. If he next leads a low trump, he should lead the fourth best of these five. Three trumps higher than the one used to trump with are marked in his hand, with the chance of his also holding a lower card than the one led.

The rule of taking the force with the fourth best, holding more than four trumps, is subject to a rather large exception. When the fourth-best trump is of such value that taking the force with it may imperil a trick later on, it must be reserved. For instance, with such cards as King, Knave, Nine, Eight, Three, a careful player would rightly trump with the Three and lead the Eight. For the time, partner is not informed as to the number of trumps held.

High Trump Led After a Force.

When, after a force, the player holds such high trumps that he has to open the suit with a high card, he leads according to the number of trumps he now holds, not according to the number originally held.

Take the case of four trumps, one of which has been used for trumping. From Queen, Knave, and two small ones the fourth best is led; from Queen, Knave, and one small one Queen is led. Hence, a player holding Queen, Knave, and two small ones, and having been forced, should lead the Queen.

With five trumps, the player who has been forced, and who then leads a high card, treats the suit as though he held only four originally. For example: with Ace, Queen, Knave, and two small ones, one having been made use of in trumping Ace, then Queen (not Knave) should be led.

The foregoing instructions assume that the trump lead is of the leader's own motion. If, for instance, his partner had called for trumps, he would follow the ordinary book rule, viz., with three trumps, trump with lowest, and lead highest; with four trumps, echo with penultimate and lead from highest downwards; with five trumps, echo with penultimate and lead lowest, except with Ace, when that card is led irrespective of number.

THE ELEVEN RULE.

To ascertain the number of cards, superior to the fourth best led, that are out against the leader, deduct the number of pips on the fourth-best card from *eleven*, and the remainder will give the number of higher cards.

PLAY OF SECOND HAND.

Low Card Led Originally.

1. Play your lowest card second hand.

It is an even chance that your partner has a higher card than the third player. You can therefore leave the trick to the third or fourth hand, without loss, and keep in your own hand any high cards you may hold over the original leader.

2. If, however, you hold certain combinations of high cards, second hand, it is in some cases advisable to play one of the high cards.

Example.—The second hand holds Queen, Knave, and a small card of the suit led. In plain suits, Ace or King must be in the third or fourth hand. Suppose the Ace is in the fourth hand, and the King in the leader's hand. If you play the Knave you win the trick, and your partner still retains the Ace. If you play the small card, it is about an even chance that your partner's Ace will be forced out, and that the King will win the second trick in the suit.

On the other hand, it is possible that the lead may have been from a long suit of small cards, and that the King is in the third hand, and the Ace in the fourth. In that case, you probably lose a trick by putting on the Knave, second hand.

It has been found by calculation, and by practical experience, that, when a small card is led, and you, second hand, hold Queen, Knave, and a small one, you will gain oftener than you will lose by playing the Knave. All other combinations of high cards, second hand, have been similarly considered, and their practical outcome is given in Table of Play of Second Hand (pp. 43, etc.).

The doubtful case is that of King and one small card, second hand. The most approved practice is to follow the general rule, and to play the low card.

3. An exception to playing the lowest, second hand, if holding one high card, unsupported by another, is when you deem it advisable to grasp at an opportunity of obtaining the lead at once. This can only happen owing to special circumstances of the hand; for these, no rule can be laid down.

Medium Card Led Originally.

4. It is to be assumed that the original lead is from a suit of four or more cards, and that when, say, a Nine, Eight, or Seven is led, the leader holds three cards higher than the one led. (*See* Table of Leads.) You should vary your play, second hand, so as to avail yourself of this assumption.

Example.—The original lead is an Eight. You, second hand, hold King, Knave, Nine, and a small card of the suit. If the Eight is a true lead, the eldest hand must hold three higher, viz., Ace, Queen, Ten. Therefore, you should not play your lowest card, second hand, but should cover the Eight with the Nine.

5. It follows that, in all instances, when you hold the dovetailing cards which complete an ascending sequence, you should cover the card led with the lowest which completes the sequence. To take an extreme example: The original lead is a Six. You hold Ace, Queen, Knave, Eight, Seven, second hand. If you can depend on an original lead from four cards, the leader must hold King, Ten, Nine. You should therefore play the Seven. (For various cases, *see* Table of Play of Second Hand, pp. 43, etc.)

The same applies to Ace led, followed by a medium card. If the eldest hand is an American leader, you know that he holds two cards higher than the medium card now led, and you should cover or pass accordingly. Thus: Ace is led; you play Five; the third hand plays Two; your partner plays Nine. Seven is next led. You, second hand. remain with King, Knave, Eight. You should play the Eight, as the leader must hold Queen and Ten.

If not an American leader, and the Six had been led, your play would be the same, as then the leader holds three cards higher than the Six.

High Card Led Originally.

6. When a Ten, or an honor, is led originally, and you, second hand, hold a card or cards higher than the one led, you ought to know, in nearly all cases, what combination of high cards the leader holds. (*See* Table of Leads.) Your play will often depend on this knowledge.

Example.—Ten is led originally. You, second hand, hold Ace, Queen, and small. It is morally certain that the lead was from King, Knave, Ten, etc. You should, therefore, play the Queen. (For other cases, *see* Table of Play of Second Hand, pp. 43, etc.)

7. If an honor is led, and you hold the Ace, put it on, second hand.

8. If an honor is led, and you hold a higher honor, not the Ace, play your lowest card, second hand.

The play, if the second hand holds an honor and only *one or two* small cards, is disputed. Thus, if Queen is led, and the second hand holds King and one or two small cards, some players cover with the King. It can, however, be shown by calculation, that the more advantageous course is to pass.

Second Round of a Suit.

9. The play of the second hand depends mainly on the fall of the cards in the first round, as the following examples will show:

Example 1.—On the first round a small card is led. You, holding King, Ten, and a small card, play the small one. Third hand plays the Queen. He, therefore, does not hold the Knave, the rule being to play the lowest of cards of equal value, or in sequence. (*See* Table of Leads.) Your partner wins with the Ace. On the second round of the suit, another small card is led through you. You, knowing that the Knave is not in the third hand, play the Ten.

If you could not tell the position of the Knave, you would generally be right to play the King (the winning card) on the second round. (*And, see* Rule 10, p. 42.)

Example 2.—On the first round a small card is led. You, holding Nine and two small ones, play the lowest. The third hand plays the Ten, which your partner wins with the Knave. The Ten is, therefore, the highest card of that suit in the third hand. (*See* Table of Leads.) If, on the second round of the suit, a card smaller than the Nine is led through you, you should put on the Nine.

Example 3.—On the first round of a suit, you play a high card, as instructed by the Table (pp. 43, etc.), and win the trick. If led through on the second round, you should generally play your next highest. Thus: With Queen, Knave, and one small card, you play the Knave, and win the trick. If a small card of the suit is led through you a second time, you should play the Queen.

10. When a medium or high card is led through you originally, you will generally know, on the second round, what other high cards the leader holds in the suit, and sometimes, whether those he does not hold are in the third hand or in the fourth hand. If you remain with a high card and a low card, you will generally be able to decide which of them to play by making use of this knowledge. And,

11. Failing indications to the contrary, play the winning card on the second round; do not play the second-best card; and, not holding the winning card, play your lowest as a rule.

In trumps, with the winning trump on the second round, and good cards in plain suits, and not being desirous of stopping the trump lead, it is sometimes advisable to pass.

Returned Leads.

12. When a suit originally led up to you, fourth hand, is returned through you, you become second hand on the second round of the suit. The rules given for the second hand, in the case of a suit led through the same player twice, do not now apply. The general rule of play is simple. Holding the winning card, play it; holding high sequence cards, generally play the lowest of them; and otherwise play lowest.

Leads Late in a Hand.

13. When a forced lead is made, the card led is generally the highest in the leader's hand. It therefore behooves you, as second hand, to do one of two things: (*a*) either to play your lowest, leaving the chance of the first trick to your partner; or (*b*) to play the winning card, or the lowest of two or more high sequence cards. No general rule can be laid down.

Playing to the Score.

14. Late in a hand, you should bear in mind how many tricks are required to win or save the game, or a point, and should play accord-

ingly. The simplest case is where one trick is required. Thus: With Ace, Queen, Knave, second hand, the lead being from a strong suit, the usual play is the Knave. But, only wanting one trick, you should, of course, play the Ace.

When not Able to Follow Suit.

15. Your play, second hand, depends on your strength in trumps. If strong in trumps, you should pass a card of a suit of which your partner may hold the highest; if weak, the best use to which you can put your trumps is to make tricks by trumping, unless you are certain that your partner can win the trick.

TABLE OF PLAY, SECOND HAND.

Note 1.—With stronger sequence cards than those tabulated, the second hand plays the lowest of the sequence. Thus:—With Ace, King, etc., he plays King; with Ace, King, Queen, etc., he plays Queen; and so on.

Note 2.—Obvious variations on account of the turn-up card are neglected. Thus:—With Ace, King, etc., Queen turned up, play lowest.

Note 3.—When calling for trumps, play the card next higher than the one indicated in the Table, if of indifferent value.

Suits Headed by Ace.

Leader.	Second Hand's Cards.	Play.
Any card.	etc.	King.

In trumps, with Ace, King, and small, and not being desirous of stopping the trump lead, nor of obtaining the lead, play lowest.

Leader.	Second Hand's Cards.	Play.
Card lower than Eight.	 etc.	King.

If Eight is led originally, play Knave (*see* Rules 4 and 5, p. 40). And similarly, with Ace, King, Ten, play Ten on Eight led; and so on.

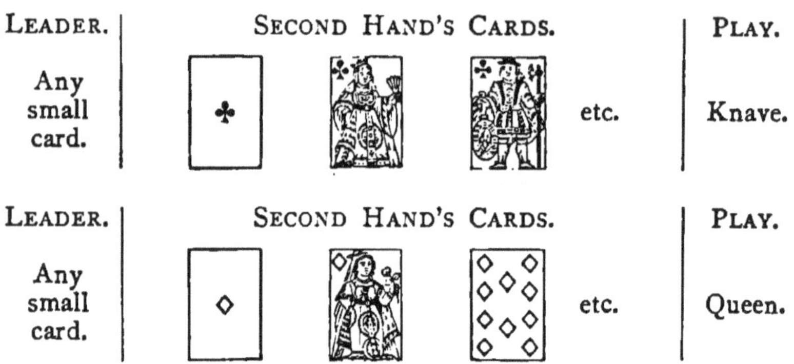

Leader.	Second Hand's Cards.	Play.
Any small card.	etc.	Knave.

Leader.	Second Hand's Cards.	Play.
Any small card.	etc.	Queen.

But play Ten *in trumps;* or *in plain suits* if strong enough in trumps to lead them; or with only three of the suit in hand.

Leader.	Second Hand's Cards.	Play.
Any card except honor.	etc.	Lowest.

With five or more in suit, play lowest if strong enough in trumps to lead them; Queen if weak.

If Knave is led, play Ace.

Leader.	Second Hand's Cards.	Play.
Any small card.	etc.	Lowest.

In trumps, play Ten.

Leader.	Second Hand's Cards.	Play.
Any card except honor.	and small.	Lowest.

If an honor is led, play Ace. But, *in trumps*, if not desirous of stopping the trump lead, nor of obtaining the lead, play lowest.

Some players, with Ace, Knave, etc., pass the King led. It is seldom good play to do so; but such play may sometimes be advisable towards the end of a hand, when the position of most of the remaining cards is known.

SUITS HEADED BY KING.

LEADER.	SECOND HAND'S CARDS.	PLAY.
Any card except Ace.	 etc.	Queen.

In trumps, with King, Queen, and more than one small (excluding the Ten), and not being desirous of stopping the trump lead, nor of obtaining the lead, play lowest.

In trumps, with King, Queen only, small card led, it is often advisable to play King.

If Knave is led originally, cover with Queen, *in trumps*. *In plain suits*, many players cover; but it can be shown by calculation that it is better to play lowest.

LEADER.	SECOND HAND'S CARDS.	PLAY.
Card lower than Eight.	etc.	Queen.

If Eight is led originally, play Ten (*see* Rules 4 and 5, p. 40). And similarly, with King, Queen, Nine, play Nine on Eight led; and so on.

LEADER.	SECOND HAND'S CARDS.	PLAY.
Any small card.	  etc.	Ten.

LEADER.	SECOND HAND'S CARDS.	PLAY.
Card lower than Eight.	  etc.	Lowest.

If Eight is led originally, play Nine (*see* Rules 4 and 5, p. 40). And similarly, with King, Knave, and small, play Knave on Nine led; and so on.

LEADER.	SECOND HAND'S CARDS.	PLAY.
Any card led.	 and small.	Lowest.

But play King, with King and one small, if Nine is led; or, with King, Nine only, if Eight is led. In other cases, do not play King second hand, with King and one small one, unless desirous of obtaining the lead.

If Queen, or Knave, is led originally, many players, with King and two small, or with King and one small, cover the honor with the King; but it can be shown by calculation that it is better to play lowest.

In trumps, if a small card is led, and the leader, to your right, has turned up the Ace, play King, holding only King and one small. Also, if you have turned up the King, and have only one small, and a small trump is led through you, play King.

SUITS HEADED BY QUEEN.

LEADER.	SECOND HAND'S CARDS.	PLAY.
Any small card.	 etc.	Ten.

LEADER.	SECOND HAND'S CARDS.	PLAY.
Any small card.	 and one small.	Knave.

With Queen, Knave, and more than one small, play lowest.

LEADER.	SECOND HAND'S CARDS.	PLAY.
Card lower than Nine.	 and small.	Lowest.

If Ten or Nine is led originally, with Queen, and only one small, play Queen.

If Knave is led originally, many players, with Queen and two small, or with Queen and one small, cover with the Queen; but it can be shown by calculation that it is better to play lowest.

In trumps, if a small card is led, and the leader, to your right, has turned up Ace or King, play Queen, holding only Queen and one small. Also, if you have turned up the Queen, and have only one small, and a small trump is led through you, play Queen.

Suits Headed by Knave.

Leader.	Second Hand's Cards.	Play.
Any small card.	 etc.	Nine.

Leader.	Second Hand's Cards.	Play.
Any small card.	 and one small.	Ten.

With Knave, Ten, and more than one small, play lowest.

Suits Headed by Ten.

Leader.	Second Hand's Cards.	Play.
Any small card.	 and one small.	Nine.

With Ten, Nine, and more than one small, play lowest.

Some players, with Ten, Nine, and one small, play small. The advantage of playing the Nine is very slight, and Nine, followed by a small card, may be mistaken for a call for trumps by a partner who is in the habit of playing the small one.

Therefore it is not advisable to play the Nine, unless your partner is a player who adopts the same rule of play.

PLAY OF THIRD HAND.

Low Card Led Originally.

1. Play your highest, third hand.

You assume that your partner has led from his strongest suit, and, if the second hand plays a card you can beat, you, third hand, play either to win the trick, or to force out a high card from the fourth hand, in hopes of establishing your partner's suit.

2. The only exceptions are: (*a*) With Ace, Queen, you play Queen, third hand; and (*b*) with cards in sequence you play the lowest of the sequence.

High Card Led Originally.

3. You can only play properly by being familiar with the combinations from which a high card is led (*see* Table of Leads, pp. 22 to 29), and by applying this knowledge to the combinations you hold.

Example 1.—Ace, then Queen, is led. You held originally King and two small ones. You know your partner remains with Knave, and only one small card of his suit. You therefore play the small card to his Queen.

Example 2.—Ace, then Knave, is led. You held originally King and two small ones. You know your partner remains with Queen, and at least two small cards of his suit. You therefore play the King to his Knave so as to unblock his long suit.

Note.—There is a risk of losing the trick by playing the King, if the fourth hand does not follow suit to the Knave; but, in the opinion of the best judges, this risk ought to be run.

4. Your play, third hand, will often depend on the *number* of cards you hold in the suit led.

Example.—Ace, then Knave is led. You held originally King and three small ones. You play a small card to the Knave. If your partner goes on with the suit, you next play the King (even if the second hand trumps), so as to unblock the suit, of which you know your partner remains with Queen and at least one small card, and the command.

Unblocking.

5. When to unblock is a difficult point in the play. In order to understand it, you must bear in mind that your partner's object in leading from a strong suit, of four or more cards, is to make tricks with the long cards of it, should he have the lead after trumps are

out. If you retain *one* card of his suit, and that card is higher than the best he has remaining, you defeat his plans.

6. No short general rule can be given for unblocking. The Table of Play of Third Hand (pp. 50, etc.) includes many cases in which unblocking should be attempted. For others, not provided for in the Table, the following may serve:—Whenever you hold one or more high cards, and *one* low card, of a suit of which you have reason to believe your partner has the long cards, consider carefully, before playing, whether you should retain the one low card, and get rid of a possible blocking card. (*See* Examples, Rules 3 and 4, page 48.)

7. All unblocking play presupposes that your partner is correct in leads. With a partner who leads irregularly, the play of the third hand is often mere guess-work. Also, unblocking play seldom applies to the trump suit, as, even if that suit is blocked, the long trumps must make eventually.

When not Able to Follow Suit.

8. When an honor is led originally, and is not covered second hand, do not trump it, even if weak in trumps. When a Ten, or even a Nine, is led originally, and is not covered second hand, pass it as a rule, unless you are weak in trumps, and are desirous of obtaining the lead.

Second Round of a Suit.

9. When your partner returns the suit you led originally, your play, third hand, depends on (*a*) the fall of the cards in the first round; (*b*) the value of the card returned; and (*c*), when in doubt, on your strength in trumps.

Example 1.—You lead a small card from Ace, Knave, and two small ones. Your partner wins with the Queen, and returns a small card of the suit. You are now third player. It would be absurd to finesse the Knave, as the King cannot be in the hand to your right.

Example 2.—You lead a small card from Ace, Ten, and two small ones. Your partner wins with the King, and returns the Knave. If you are strong in trumps, pass it; if weak in trumps, play the Ace. And, as a general rule,

10. It is advisable, on the second round of a suit, to finesse against one card which may be to your right, if you are strong enough to lead trumps, should the finesse succeed.

11. When you are not the original leader, your play, third hand, on the second round of a suit, depends on (*a*) the previous fall of

the cards; (*b*) your knowledge of the combination led from; and (*c*) whether you desire to unblock.

Example 1.—Queen is led originally by your partner; taken fourth hand by the King. Your partner, on next obtaining the lead, leads Knave, showing that his suit consisted of at most four cards (*see* Table of Leads, pp. 22 to 29). You, remaining with Ace and one small one, should pass.

On the other hand, if your partner continues with the Ten, instead of the Knave, you should put on the Ace, in order to unblock, as your partner remains with Knave and at least two small cards (*see* Table of Leads, pp. 22 to 29).

Example 2.—You hold Ace, Queen, and a small one, of a suit of which your partner leads the Ten, originally. You, knowing the lead to be from King, Knave, Ten, etc., play the small one. Your partner continues with a small card. You should now play the Ace, not the Queen, as, if you retain the Ace, you block your partner's suit.

TABLE OF PLAY, THIRD HAND.

NOTE 1.—The Table assumes original leads from strong suits, as laid down in Table of Leads (pp. 22 to 29). The play of the third hand to forced leads depends on judgment, and cannot be tabulated.

NOTE 2.—The play of small cards to the first round is also assumed. If, in actual play, the third hand sees that he is practically in the position given in the Table, owing to the fall of high cards, or to his holding stronger cards than those mentioned, he should play accordingly.

ACE LEADS.

LEADER.	THIRD HAND'S CARDS.	PLAY.
Ace then Queen.	 and two or more small.	Small then small.

LEADER.	THIRD HAND'S CARDS.	PLAY.
Ace then Knave.	 and two small.	Small then King.

If second hand does not follow suit to the Knave, play small.
With King, and more than two small, play small to Knave.
In trumps, play small to Knave, irrespective of number.

LEADER.	THIRD HAND'S CARDS.	PLAY.
Ace then Ten.	 and two small.	Small then King.

If second hand does not follow suit to the Ten, still play King, even though second hand trumps.

With King, and more than two small, play small to Ten.

In trumps, play small to Ten, irrespective of number.

LEADER.	THIRD HAND'S CARDS.	PLAY.
Ace then Nine.	 and two small.	Small then Queen.

If second hand plays King to the Nine, still play Queen.

If second hand does not follow suit to the Nine, play Queen; but, if second hand trumps, play small.

With Queen, and more than two small, play small to Nine.

In trumps, play small to Nine, irrespective of number.

LEADER.	THIRD HAND'S CARDS.	PLAY.
Ace then honor or Ten.	None of the suit after Ace.	Small of weak plain suit.

Unless second hand covers.

LEADER.	THIRD HAND'S CARDS.	PLAY.
Ace then any card.	  and two small.	Small then Queen.

If second hand trumps the second card led, still play Queen. And, third round of the suit, play King.

With King, Queen, and more than two small, play small to Nine led after Ace.

In trumps, play Queen second round, irrespective of number.

LEADER.	THIRD HAND'S CARDS.	PLAY.
Ace then any card.	 and two small.	Small then Knave.

Even though second hand plays King.

And, whenever the third hand has four of the suit originally, and remains, on the second round, with two high cards and a low one, he should play as directed in this and the previous case.

When Ace is led originally, the third hand, with four of the suit, should begin to unblock on the first round. Thus: With King, Queen, Knave, and one small card, he should play the Knave to the Ace, and the Queen to the second round, even if the second hand trumps. For details of similar positions for unblocking with four of a suit, complete treatises must be consulted.

KING LEADS.

LEADER.	THIRD HAND'S CARDS.	PLAY.
King then Knave.	♣ and two or more small.	Small then small.

LEADER.	THIRD HAND'S CARDS.	PLAY.
King then Ten.	◇ and two small.	Small then Ace.

If second hand does not follow suit to the Ten, still play Ace, even though second hand trumps.

With Ace and three small, continue to play small.

With Ace and more than three small, play small to three rounds, and win the fourth round with the Ace.

In trumps, play small, then small, irrespective of number.

LEADER.	THIRD HAND'S CARDS.	PLAY.
King then small.	  and one small.	Small then Ace.

If second hand does not follow suit to the small card, play Knave.

With Ace, Knave, and more than one small, play Knave to the second round, unless trumped, when play small.

With Ace, Knave, only, *in plain suits*, play Knave to King led.

In trumps, with Ace, Knave only, take King with Ace, and return Knave.

Leader.	Third Hand's Cards.	Play.
King.	None of the suit.	Small of weak plain suit.

Unless second hand plays Ace.

Queen Leads.

Leader.	Third Hand's Cards.	Play.
Queen.	  and one small.	King and lead Ace.

If second hand does not follow suit, play small.

With Ace, King, and more than one small, play small (and *see* below for subsequent play).

In trumps, play small, irrespective of number.

Leader.	Third Hand's Cards.	Play.
Queen.	 and one or more small.	Small.

Unless second hand plays King.

If second hand does not follow suit, and does not trump, play Ace; unless holding Knave or Ten, with or without others, when pass or play small. And,

In trumps, play small.

Leader.	Third Hand's Cards.	Play.
Queen.	None of the suit.	Small of weak plain suit.

Unless second hand covers.

LEADER.	THIRD HAND'S CARDS.	PLAY.
Queen then Knave.	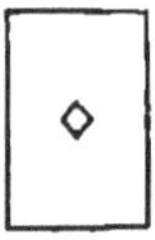  and two or more small.	Small then small.

LEADER.	THIRD HAND'S CARDS.	PLAY.
Queen then Knave.	 and two or more small.	Small then small.

The same with Ace, and two or more small, unless King is played second hand.

LEADER.	THIRD HAND'S CARDS.	PLAY.
Queen then Ten or Nine.	  and two small.	Small then King.

If second hand does not follow suit to the Ten, or Nine, still play King, even though second hand trumps.

With Ace, King, more than two small, play small to Ten or Nine.

In trumps, play small to Ten, or Nine, irrespective of number.

LEADER.	THIRD HAND'S CARDS.	PLAY.
Queen then Ten or Nine.	 and two small.	Small then King.

If second hand does not follow suit to the Ten, play small; but if second hand does not follow suit to the Nine, still play King, even though second hand trumps.

With King, and more than two small, play small to Ten, or Nine.

In trumps, play small to Ten or Nine, irrespective of number.

The same with Ace, and two or more small, unless King is played on Queen led. Also, if Queen wins the first trick, and Ten or Nine is next led, and is not covered, of course the third hand should not put on the Ace.

LEADER.	THIRD HAND'S CARDS.	PLAY.
Queen then small.	  and one small.	Small then Ace.

If second hand trumps the small card, play Knave.

With Ace, Knave, and more than one small, play small, then Knave.

In trumps, play small, then Knave, irrespective of number.

KNAVE LEADS.

LEADER.	THIRD HAND'S CARDS.	PLAY.
Knave.	   and one small.	Queen and lead King.

Even if second hand trumps; and, second round, play King.

With Ace, King, Queen, and more than one small, play small.

In trumps, play small, irrespective of number.

LEADER.	THIRD HAND'S CARDS.	PLAY.
Knave.	  and one or more small.	King.

If strong in trumps, play small, unless second hand covers.

If second hand trumps, play small.

In trumps, play small, unless second hand covers.

LEADER.	THIRD HAND'S CARDS.	PLAY.
Knave.	  and one or more small.	Small.

Unless second hand covers.

If second hand does not follow suit, and does not trump, play Ace.

In trumps, if second hand does not follow suit, play small.

LEADER.	THIRD HAND'S CARDS.	PLAY.
Knave.	  and one small.	Queen.

Even though second hand plays Ace. And, second round, play King.

If second hand does not follow suit to the Knave, play small.

With King, Queen, and more than one small, play small.

In trumps, play small, irrespective of number.

LEADER.	THIRD HAND'S CARDS.	PLAY.
Knave.	 and one small.	Ace.

If second hand trumps, play small.

If second hand does not follow suit, and does not trump, the play of the third hand depends on whether the lead is from Knave, Ten, Nine, or from King, Queen, Knave. If the former, play Ace; if the latter, pass. To decide this, the leader's habit is the main guide (*see* Table of Leads, pp. 22 to 29).

With Ace and more than one small, play small, unless second hand covers (and *see* below for subsequent play). If second hand does not follow suit, play as directed in previous paragraph.

LEADER.	THIRD HAND'S CARDS.	PLAY.
Knave.	 and one or more small.	Small.

Unless second hand plays Queen.

LEADER.	THIRD HAND'S CARDS.	PLAY.
Knave.	None of the suit.	Small of weak plain suit.

Unless second hand covers.

LEADER.	THIRD HAND'S CARDS.	PLAY.
Knave then King or Queen.	 and two small.	Small then Ace.

If second hand does not follow suit to the King led (after Knave), play small; but, if second hand does not follow suit to the Queen, still play Ace, even though second hand trumps.

With Ace, and more than two small, play small, then small.

In trumps, play small, then small, irrespective of number.

If Knave led is followed by Ten, the third hand, whatever his cards, does not attempt to unblock. If Knave led is followed by Nine, or Eight, the third hand should play to unblock, on the same lines as when Queen is followed by Ten, or Nine, bearing in mind that there is one other high card to be accounted for. Thus: With King, Queen, and two small, if Knave led is followed by Nine, the third hand should play Queen, to Nine, in plain suits, and third round should play King.

TEN LEADS.

LEADER.	THIRD HAND'S CARDS.	PLAY.
Ten.	  only.	Ace and lead Queen.

If second hand trumps, play Queen.

LEADER.	THIRD HAND'S CARDS.	PLAY.
Ten.	 and one or more small.	Ace.

Unless second hand trumps.

LEADER.	THIRD HAND'S CARDS.	PLAY.
Ten.	 and one or more small,	Small.

LEADER.	THIRD HAND'S CARDS.	PLAY.
Ten.	None of the suit.	Small of weak plain suit.

Unless weak in trumps, and desirous of obtaining the lead; or, unless second hand covers.

LEADER.	THIRD HAND'S CARDS.	PLAY.
Ten then small.	  ♣ and one small.	Small then Ace.

If second hand trumps the small card, still play Ace. With Ace, Queen, and two small, play small, then Queen; but, if second hand trumps, play small, then small. On the third round, if leader plays small, third hand should play Ace.

With Ace, Queen, and more than two small, if second hand trumps, continue to play small.

In trumps, play small, then Queen, irrespective of number.

NINE LEADS.

With Ace, Queen only, play Ace, and lead Queen.

With Ace, Queen, and one or two small, play Queen to Nine. With more than two small, pass the Nine if strong in trumps.

With King, Queen, etc., the obvious play is the Queen; and with Ace, or King, and any number of small cards, the Ace or King.

With Queen, or Knave, and one, two, or three small ones, play Queen or Knave; but, with more than three small, pass the Nine, if strong in trumps.

With none of the suit pass the Nine, unless weak in trumps, and desirous of obtaining the lead.

PLAY OF FOURTH HAND.

The fourth player having, with a few exceptions, merely to win the trick, if against him, his play involves no further development of general principles.

The exceptional cases, where the fourth hand should not win the trick, though he can, or should win his partner's trick in order to get the lead depends so much on the previous fall of the cards, that they can only be determined by the judgment of the player.

MANAGEMENT OF TRUMPS.

Lead Trumps when very Strong in Them.

With five or more trumps you are very strong. You should lead them with the object of exhausting the adversaries' trumps. With five trumps your chance of succeeding in this and remaining with the long trumps is considerable, and you have an excellent prospect of bringing in any long suit which you or your partner may hold.

Number being the principal element of strength, you should not be deterred from leading from five trumps simply because the fourth hand has turned up an honor. Nor should you lead from less than five trumps merely because an honor has been turned up second hand.

If you are very strong in trumps (*i. e.*, with a minimum of five trumps, one being an honor, or four trumps, two being honors), and have not the lead you can *ask for trumps* (*i. e.*, call on your partner to lead a trump), by playing an unnecessarily high card before a low one. Thus, if your partner leads King, Ace of a suit, and to the first round you play the Three, to the second round the Two, you have asked for trumps. Your partner is then bound to relinquish his game, and to lead trumps at once. If he has three trumps he should lead his highest, and then his next highest. If he has more than three trumps, his lowest, unless he has the Ace, when he should lead that, and then his lowest (*see* p. 63).

If your partner leads trumps or asks for trumps, and you have four or more trumps, you should *echo* by asking at the first opportunity (*see* p. 64).

You should lead from four trumps if you get the lead after the adversaries' hands are cleared of your strong suit, or so far cleared that you command it.

As a rule you should not lead from less than four trumps unless:

You have winning cards in every suit; or

The adversaries are both trumping; or

The game is hopeless unless your partner proves strong.

You should at once return your partner's trump lead, because he, by leading trumps, declares a strong game, and it is your best policy to second him, even if by so doing you abandon your own plans.

DO NOT FORCE YOUR PARTNER IF YOU ARE WEAK IN TRUMPS.

With less than four trumps you are weak. When weak yourself, you should not lead a card for your partner to trump; for, by forcing, you weaken him and run the serious risk of leaving the command of trumps with the adversaries.

Exceptions.—You may force your partner though yourself weak:

If he has already been forced, and has not afterwards led a trump; or

If you know him to be weak in trumps, as by his having trumped second hand; or

If you and he can each trump a different suit; or

When one trick from his hand wins or saves the game or a point.

The same considerations which make it inexpedient to force your partner when you are weak, show that it is advantageous to

FORCE A STRONG TRUMP HAND OF THE ADVERSARY.

For you thereby take the best chance of preventing his making use of his trumps for bringing in a suit. If he refuses to take a force, keep on giving it to him.

For instance, if he passes your King (led from King, Queen, etc.), and the King wins, continue the suit, and so on. Weak players never understand this; they do not like to see their winning cards trumped, and therefore frequently lead trumps when an adversary refuses to be forced.

It now hardly requires to be stated that it is bad play intentionally to force a weak adversary, and still worse to lead a suit to which both adversaries renounce, as the weak will trump, and the strong get rid of a losing card.

PLAY THE LOWEST OF A SEQUENCE WHEN NOT LEADING.

You naturally win a trick with the smallest card you can, or if you cannot win it, you throw away the smallest you have. By adopting a uniform plan, you enable your partner to tell what cards you hold. And it is found by experience that this information is of more value to your partner than to the adversaries.

KEEP THE COMMAND OF YOUR ADVERSARIES' SUIT; GET RID OF THE COMMAND OF YOUR PARTNER'S SUIT.

You assume that the suit chosen for the lead by each player is his strong suit. By leading the winning card of a suit you assist in clearing it. This, of course, is to your advantage so far as your partner's suit is concerned. But the reverse holds with regard to your opponents' suits. Here you want to obstruct the establishment of a suit as much as you can, and should therefore not only refrain from leading the commanding cards, but should keep second best and third best cards guarded with small ones, as long as you can.

If, however, the adversaries continue their suit, you should, as a rule, play the winning card of it in the second round, as the chances are it will be trumped third round.

This is the simplest rule for beginners. But there are various exceptions. Thus, if you have best and third best of a suit, and have reason to suppose the second best is to your right, you would play the third best. In trumps, also, if you are not desirous of stopping the trump lead at once, it is often right to pass the second round.

Discard from your Weakest Suit.

When not able to follow suit, you do no harm by throwing away from suits in which you are already weak; but if you throw away from a strong suit, you diminish its numerical power.

The same rule applies as to trumping second hand. If weak in trumps, trump a doubtful card, but not if strong.

There is one exception to the rule of discarding from the weakest suit. If the opponents declare great strength in trumps, as by leading or asking for them, you have no reasonable chance of bringing in a long suit. In such cases you must play on the defense, and guard your weak suits, discarding from your best protected suit, which is generally your long suit.

It follows, if your partner pursues this plan, that he will give you credit for weakness in the suit you first discard, when no great adverse strength in trumps has been shown, and he will refrain from subsequently leading that suit. But, if great adverse strength in trumps has been declared, he will assume you to be strong in the suit you first discard, and will lead that suit unless he has a very strong suit of his own.

Play to the Score.

All general rules are subject to this one. Thus, if one trick saves or wins the game, make it at once. For example: The score is Love-all; you have four tricks; the adversaries have shown two by honors; your partner opens a fresh suit of which you have Ace, Queen. The general rule is to play the Queen; but, as here one trick saves the game, you would generally be right to play the Ace.

The example is given for one trick; but you should always keep in mind how many tricks are requisite to win or save the game, or even a point, and play accordingly.

Watch the Fall of the Cards.

By observing the suits led by the different players, and the value of the cards played by each, and by counting the number of cards out in the various suits, especially in trumps, you will find that you will often know the position of all the important cards remaining in; and by means of this knowledge you will be enabled to play the hand, particularly toward its close, to the best advantage. You should begin by recording in your own mind the broad indications of the hand as it progresses; you will gradually acquire the power of noting even the minor features without any great effort.

You should draw your inferences *at the time*. Thus, if a King is led originally and you have the Ace of that suit, you should *at once* infer that the leader has the Queen; and so on for other combinations.

The following table gives some of the more important inferences:

Table.

PLAY.	INFERENCE.
Original Leader.	
Suit led.	Is his strongest.
Small card led.	Has not any combination from which a high card is led.
Ace led.	Has at least five in suit and has not King.
Ace then Queen.	Has Knave.
King led.	Has Ace or Queen, or both.
Queen led.	Has not Ace or King, but almost certainly Knave and Ten.
And so on through the whole list of leads.	
Plain suit led originally.	Is not very strong in trumps.
Leader, Second Round of a Suit.	
Does not lead winning card.	Has not got it.
Leads the second best.	Has the third best.
Returns partner's lead with a low card; afterwards plays a higher one.	Has more.
Returns partner's lead with a high card; afterwards plays a lower one.	Has no more.

PLAY.	INFERENCE.
SECOND HAND.	
Plays a low card.	His lowest, unless calling for trumps.
Plays a high card.	Has no more, or the next highest, or one of the combinations with which a high card is played second hand.
THIRD HAND.	
Plays Ace.	Has neither King nor Queen.
FOURTH HAND.	
Does not win the trick if against him.	Has no higher card than the one against him.
Wins with any card.	Has no card between the one he plays and the one against him.
SECOND, THIRD, OR FOURTH PLAYER.	
Any card.	Has not the one next below it.
Does not cover or win the trick.	Card played is his lowest, unless he is asking for trumps.
Any suit discarded.	Is weak in that suit, except great strength in trumps has been declared against him, when he is strong.
TRUMPS.	
Leads to force his partner.	Is strong in trumps, unless partner has already been forced accidentally and has not led trumps.
Refrains from forcing his partner.	Is weak in trumps.
Does not trump a winning card.	Has no trump or has four trumps and wants trumps led.
Trumps a doubtful card.	Is weak in trumps.
Does not trump a doubtful card.	Is strong in trumps, or has no trumps.
Plays unnecessarily a high card before a low one in any suit.	Is calling for trumps.

ASKING FOR TRUMPS.

This "ask" is indicated by your playing an unnecessarily high card; that is, on a trick won by Ace, third in hand, you as fourth player throw the Six, and next round play the Two, or, as second player, play the Four, and then next round, drop the Two or Three. Thus asking for trumps means playing a *totally unnecessarily* high card, when by subsequent play you show you could have played a lower card. You must be careful to distinguish between a totally unnecessarily high card, and a card played to cover another card, or to protect your partner. If you hold Knave, Ten, and Two of a suit, as second player, you play your Ten, on next round you would play your Two, if this trick was won by a card higher than your Knave. Your partner must not assume, from the fall of the Two, that you have asked for trumps; you have simply played the proper card. If you wished to ask for trumps, with this hand you should play your Knave on the first card led. But your partner cannot tell until the third round of the suit whether you have or have not asked for trumps under the above conditions. Thus the play of the second hand must be watched carefully to note whether the card played is, or is not, a protecting card, and not an "ask". With fourth player there is less chance of mistake, for if the trick be already won, and he throws a Five or any other higher card, and next round plays the Two or Three, it must be an "ask". If the card led by the original leader be a high card, such as King or Ace, then the play of second player is not liable to be misunderstood. No player can ask for trumps by his lead.

THE ECHO.

As a sequel to the "ask for trumps", another system of play has been for some time adopted, by which, if your partner ask for trumps, you can inform him whether you hold four, or more or less than four trumps; that is, either to "ask" in trumps when they are led, or ask in some other suit after your partner has asked. This echo is a most powerful aid, as it is almost certain to enable you to win an extra trick. The following may serve as an example:

Your partner holds Ace, King, Queen, and Ten of trumps; you hold Nine, Five, Three, and Two. Your partner has asked for trumps, and immediately after leads the Queen. On this you play your Three. He then leads King; on this you play your Two. He then knows you hold four trumps. He then leads Ace, on which you play your Five, and Knave falls from one adversary. Your partner now holds best trump, and could draw the remaining trump if it were in the adversary's hand; but you by the echo have told him it is in your hand. Had you not echoed, your partner would draw this trump, as he would conclude it was held by the adversaries.

DUPLICATE WHIST.

KALAMAZOO METHOD.*

Duplicate Whist is in no sense a new game; its only distinguishing feature is that the hands for the whole evening, or sitting, after having been once played, are played over again, or in duplicate. In the duplicate play, each player plays the hand that one of his opponents originally held. With this in mind, all misconception in relation to further details will be avoided.

Below is described an exceedingly simple and convenient device by means of which the duplicate play of any number of hands is accomplished.

FACE OF TRAY.

The above is a cut of a Whist tray. The tray is made of tar board or other suitable material covered with cloth or leather. Its size is 10 inches long, 9 inches wide. A rubber band extends from the middle of each side to a point directly toward the center of the

* Copied by permission of Messrs. Ihling, Bros. & Everard, Kalamazoo, proprietors of the patent.

tray. Only the ends of the band are fastened to the tray, allowing the middle portion to be raised above the tray and a hand of cards to be slipped under the band and held between it and the tray. In the center of the tray is an index pointing directly toward one side of the tray. Near one side of the tray are two stars.

How the Tray is Used.

The tray is placed in the center of the table with the side containing the stars toward the north. In this position the index in the center of the tray points to the player who is to lead, and therefore the immediately preceding player must deal. The trump is not turned, but one suit is declared trump for the evening. After the cards have been dealt, first player plays by laying his card face up on the table, placing it immediately in front of him, instead of in the center of the table. In turn the other players now play in the same way. The side winning the trick takes a poker chip from the center of table. (There should be thirteen chips in center of the tray representing the number of tricks.) Each succeeding round is played in like manner, the winner of the immediately preceding trick having the lead as in ordinary Whist. The cards of each round should be so placed as to exactly cover those of the preceding round, otherwise the cards of each round should be turned face down after the round has been completed.

After the hands of the first deal have been played each player takes up the hand he has just played, shuffles it, and slips it face down under the rubber band on his side of the tray. The chips are counted, and the result of the hand is then scored as described below. The tray is laid aside and another placed on the table with the side containing the stars toward the north, as before. Of course another deck of cards is necessary with which to make a new deal. Any desired number of trays having been thus used, they are returned to the table singly, bearing the original hands, which are now played over again. In returning a tray to the table, the side containing the stars is placed to the east or west. This accomplishes the exchange of hands, that is, gives to each player the hand that one of his opponents held originally. The index in the center of the tray locates the lead in the play of both originals and duplicates.

For convenience in keeping the score and for the purpose of comparing corresponding results of the original and duplicate play the trays are numbered 1, 2, 3, etc. The number is on the under side of the tray.

The duplicates are returned to the tables in irregular order, not consecutively; the numbers on the under side of the trays are not to be referred to by the players until the deal is played out. By this irregular return of the duplicates the players will not know which deal is before them, until reference is made to the number of the tray for scoring, consequently any recollection of the deal from the first play will be impossible.

THE SCORE.

The score may be kept in any of the usual ways, but the score-card on the following page will show the method recommended for Duplicate Whist.

The numbers in the central column correspond to the numbers on the trays. On the left of this central column are columns for scoring the number of tricks won with both the original and duplicate hands by the players occupying the north and south sides of the table. The names of these players should be written in the blank spaces left for them above the columns. The columns on the right of the central column should be used for the score of the other two players. The players who score the greatest number of tricks during the whole play are accounted the winners.

It is well known that in the ordinary seven-point game of Whist one side may win the most games while the opponents make the most points; but it is not so well known, perhaps, that one side may make the most points while the opponents win the most tricks.

TWO OR MORE TABLES.

It is evident that the same set of trays will accommodate two or more tables. Table 1 may play tray 1 and table 2 may play tray 2 at the same time. Then table 1 may play tray 2 and table 2 tray 1 at the same time. After each table has thus played trays 1 and 2, in the same way each may play trays 3 and 4, 5 and 6, etc.

If there are three tables, tables 1, 2, and 3 may play trays 1, 2, and 3, respectively, at the same time. Then tray 1 may pass to table 2; tray 2 to table 3, and tray 3 to table 1. After the three trays have been played in these positions, tray 1 may pass to table 3; tray 2 to table 1, and tray 3 to table 2. This method can be pursued until each of the three tables has played any number of times three trays.

In a manner entirely analogous, four tables can play any number of times four trays; five tables, any number of times five trays; six tables, any number of times six trays; etc.

Score Sheet for Duplicate Whist.

Table No. .... *Date,* *189*

.....................N. *vs.* ....E.

.....................S. ....W.

SCORE NUMBER OF TRICKS MADE BY EACH SIDE.

Original Score.	Duplicate Score.	Total.	No. of Deal.	Original Score.	Duplicate Score.	Total.
			1			
			2			
			3			
			4			
			5			
			6			
			7			
			8			
			9			
			10			
			11			
			12			
			13			
			14			
			15			
			16			
			17			
			18			
			19			
			20			

With a limited number, say 2 to 4 tables, some one of the players, usually the host or hostess, performs the duty of passing and caring for the trays. To avoid confusion, one person should have entire charge of this service, neither soliciting nor accepting assistance from anybody else, and it is better, when convenient, to have this duty assigned to a person not in the play.

In Duplicate Whist very interesting contests between different clubs are easily arranged; any Whist company may be divided by lot, or by choice of two leaders, into two sides, and the result decided by the aggregate scores at all the tables. As an additional feature prizes may be awarded to the couple having the highest score.

Rules for Duplicate Whist.

Duplicate Whist is subject to the laws of the regular game in all cases except the following:

In the penalty incurred for a revoke, etc., the necessary points are deducted from the defaulter's score, and added to the opponents'; but the points can in no case exceed the number of tricks taken in that hand by the offending party, so that the limit of thirteen for one hand shall not be exceeded.

Again: If a player makes a misdeal, he must deal again, without incurring any penalty for it.

Special Caution.

When more tables than one take part, do not make any comparison of scores until the game is over.

Cards should not be thrown down, claiming remainder of tricks because holding winning cards, but *hands should be played through*, one trick at a time.

When a deal is played through, each player should immediately place his packet of thirteen cards in its place on the tray, before the scorers count and score the result.

DUPLICATE WHIST WITHOUT TRAYS.

Duplicate Whist may be played without the assistance of the trays, as follows: A, B, C, and D play against W, X, Y, and Z,—A and B *vs.* W and X in room No. 1, and C and D *vs.* Y and Z in room No. 2, sitting as represented in the diagram:

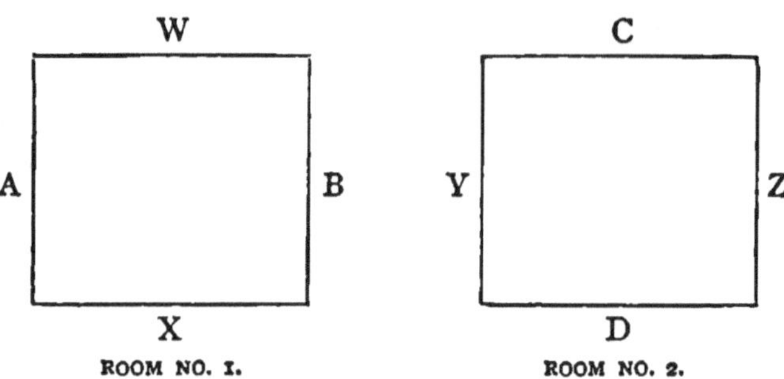

ROOM NO. 1. ROOM NO. 2.

The deal starts at the same side of the table in each room, say A in No. 1 and Y in No. 2.

After the hand has been played, and scored, as already described, A and B, W and X go to room No. 2, where a similar process has been going on; C, D, Y, Z, of course, going to room No. 1. A occupies Y's seat, B takes Z's seat, W takes C's seat, and X takes D's seat, similarly Y takes A's seat in room No. 1, Z takes B's seat, C takes W's seat, and D takes the seat vacated by X. Thus each player plays the hand held originally by one of his adversaries.

After the play of the hand is completed, and the score marked, the cards are thrown in the center of the table as at ordinary Whist. A new deal ensues, and after being played the teams again reverse, thus resuming their original positions, and the play continues as before.

DUMMY WHIST.

This is played by three players.

One hand, called Dummy's, lies exposed on the table.

The laws are the same as those of Whist, with these exceptions:

I. Dummy deals at the commencement of each rubber.

II. Dummy is not liable to the penalty for a revoke, as his adversaries see his cards; should he revoke and the error not be discovered until the trick is turned and quitted, it stands good, and the hand proceeds as though the revoke had not been discovered.

If Dummy's partner revoke, he is liable to the usual penalties.

III. Dummy being blind and deaf, his partner is not liable to any penalty for an error whence he can gain no advantage. Thus, he may expose some or all of his cards—or may declare that he has the game, or trick, etc., without incurring any penalty; if, however, he lead from Dummy's hand when he should lead from his own, or *vice versâ*, a suit may be called from the hand which ought to have led.

The whole policy of the assailants' game consists in leading through Dummy's strong suits, and up to the weak; the return of partner's lead being, in most cases, a secondary consideration.

This game eminently displays the rationale of some of the most important maxims at Whist; for example:

The expediency of leading a strengthening card to partner.

The benefit of pursuing an old suit in preference to a fresh weak one.

The importance of *placing* the lead.

The mischief of forcing the strong and weak hand indiscriminately; and the proper application of a thirteenth card.

The policy of retaining the command of the adversaries' suit.

DOUBLE DUMMY.

Is played by two players, each having a Dummy or exposed hand for his partner. The laws of the game do not differ from Dummy Whist, except in the following special Law: There is no misdeal, as the deal is a disadvantage.

Each player and the two Dummies take the deal in turn, and are liable to all the laws previously stated.

Although cards will "beat their makers", the game of Double Dummy is more in favor of the best player than any other at Whist.

It undoubtedly is very instructive to the novice, and has been recommended by high authorities as the best mode of studying the game.

THE AMERICAN WHIST CODE.

The code adopted by "The American Whist League" differs from the English Whist Laws very materially. It is not, however, thought advisable to give the American laws here, because it is generally understood that the League intends to perfect the code at the next meeting of the Congress, and, if possible, render subsequent amendment unnecessary. The following are, at present, the principal points of difference between the two codes:

I. The American game consists of seven points. *Singles*, *doubles*, and *the rubber*, together with scoring by honors, have all been abolished.

II. The English Law 84, which provides for the consultation of partners as to penalty, has been expunged, and gives to the player on the right of the offending party authority to exact the penalty (*see* Law 38, American code).

III. The American code provides that only a single penalty can be exacted for leading out of turn. The penalty adopted is calling a suit from either of the adversaries when it is their turn to lead (*see* Law 38, American code).

IV. No one is permitted to examine a trick after it is turned and quitted.

V. The American laws do not allow a player to ask his renouncing partner whether he has none of the suit led; or to inquire what the trump suit is.

VI. The trump card may be left on the table until just previous to the turning and quitting of the second trick.

VII. The phraseology of the English laws has been greatly improved, and the number reduced from 91 to 61. The laws relating to exposed cards are both comprehensive and clear, and are a great improvement on the English laws framed for the same purpose. Law 61 provides that "no conversation shall be indulged in during the play of the hand except such as is required or permitted by the foregoing rules". The whole code seems to aim at promoting silence during play.

Dick & Fitzgerald

PUBLISHERS,

18 ANN STREET,

POST OFFICE BOX 2975. NEW YORK.

Upon receipt of the price, any books advertised in the following pages will be sent by mail postage paid, to any Post Office in the United States, Canada, and the Universal Postal Union.

No Books Exchanged. **No Books sent C. O. D.**

Not Responsible for Money or Books sent by Mail, unless Registered.

Parcels will be registered on receipt of Ten Cents in addition to the amount of the order.

Under no Circumstances will Books be sent Subject to Approval.

No Orders whatever will be Filled unless sufficient money accompanies them.

Write your name plainly.

Give full Address, with Post Office, County and State.

A complete descriptive Catalogue will be mailed free on application.

HOW TO SEND MONEY.

In remitting by mail the safest means are a Post-office or Express Money Order, or a Draft on a New York Bank, payable to Dick & Fitzgerald. When these are not procurable, Cash (or a Postal Note) should be sent in a Registered Letter. Unused United States Postage Stamps, of the denomination of Ten Cents or under, will be taken as cash in amounts less than One Dollar. Soiled Stamps, Postage Stamps other than those of the United States, and personal checks or drafts on local banks cannot be accepted

The American Hoyle; or, Gentleman's Hand-book of Games. By "Trumps". This work, which has already passed through FOURTEEN EDITIONS, has long since been accorded the position of an exclusive authority on games played in America.

The fifteenth edition, now issued, newly arranged, in new type, and in a great measure re-written, contains all the latest novelties, as well as the recent changes in games already in vogue, some of them being profusely illustrated.

Among the new games introduced in this edition are Rubicon Piquet, Rubicon Bézique, Grabouche, Solo Whist, Cayenne Whist, Domino Whist, etc.

In the game of Whist, the new features are "Cavendish's" rules for play, with best leads, and a critical examination of the system of "American Leads", with directions for the play of second and third hands, elucidated by card illustrations; also, the mode of procedure in Duplicate Whist.

The various games of Billiards and Pool, with the modern rules adopted in the latest matches and tournaments, are inserted by special permission accorded by the Brunswick-Balke-Collender Company.

The games of Draw Poker, including Jack-pots; also Baccarat Banque and Baccarat Chemin de Fer, have been carefully remodeled and corrected.

The work also includes an elaborate exposition of the Doctrine of Chances, as applied to the occurrence and recurrence of possibilities in all matters connected with games of chance. 514 pages.
Library Edition, 12mo., cloth $1.50
A cheaper edition, 16mo., in paper covers .... 50 cts.
Bound in boards .... 75 cts.

Dick's Hand-book of Cribbage. Containing full directions for playing all the Varieties of the Game, and the Laws which govern them. This work is ENTIRELY NEW, and gives the correct method of playing the Six-Card, Five-Card, Two-Handed, Three-Handed, and Four-Handed varieties of the Game, with instructive examples, showing clearly all the combinations of Hand, Crib, and Play, with a thorough investigation of long sequences in play, and the value of Hands. The Laws of the Game have been carefully revised in accordance with the recognized usages of the present time, and constitute a reliable authority on all points of the Game. 18mo., cloth, flexible .... 50 cts.

Dick's Games of Patience; or, Solitaire with Cards. New and Revised Edition. Containing Sixty-four Games. Illustrated with Fifty explanatory full-page Tableaux. This treatise on Solitaire embraces a number of new and original Games, and all the Games of Patience at present in favor with the most experienced players. Each game is carefully and lucidly described, with the distinctive rules to be observed and hints as to the best means of success in play. The Tableaux furnish efficient aid in rendering the disposition of the cards necessary to each game plain and easily comprehensible. The difficulty usually attending descriptions of intricate games is reduced, as far as possible, by precision in method and terseness of expression in the text, and the illustrations serve to dispel any possible ambiguity that might be unavoidable without their aid. Quarto, 143 pages.

Board covers.................................... 75 cts.
Cloth.................................... $1.00

Modern Whist. A Treatise on the Game of Whist, introducing all the modern methods and usages of the scientific game, mainly derived from the latest works of "Cavendish", the leading authority in all that pertains to the game of Whist.

The most advantageous leads, according to "Cavendish", as well as the system of "American Leads", are given in detail, including a critical analysis, with Tables and Illustrations, of the best play for second and third hands.

This treatise contains all the instruction necessary to make an expert modern Whist player. Paper covers............ 25 cts.

Pole on Whist. The Theory of the Modern Scientific Game of Whist. By William Pole, F.R.S. This complete and exhaustive Treatise on the Game is in handy form for the pocket, and affords lucid instructions at all stages of the Game for partners to play in combination for their best interests.................... 20 cts.

American Leads at Whist. A condensed Treatise abridged from the well-known work by "Cavendish", explaining and elucidating the generally accepted modern methods of American Leads as applied to legitimate signaling between partners during the progress of the game. Illustrated with Diagrams. Vest pocket size..15 cts.

Cinch. A thorough hand-book of the game of Cinch, containing the correct method of playing, and the Laws which govern it; compiled from the best and most reliable authorities. By "Trumps".................................... 10 cts.

Hoyle's Games. By "Trumps". A Complete Manual of the games of skill and chance as played in America, and an acknowledged "arbiter on all disputed points"; thoroughly revised and corrected in accordance with the latest and best authorities.

It contains the modern laws and complete instructions for the games of Chess, Draughts, Dominoes, Dice, Backgammon, and Billiards, as well as all the games with cards at present in vogue, including the more recently introduced methods of playing Baccarat, Duplicate Whist, Cayenne Whist, Hearts, Grabouche Newmarket, Solo Whist, and Five and Nine or Domino Whist, etc. Profusely illustrated with explanatory card engravings, and diagrams. 16mo., 514 pages, cloth.................. $1.25

Bound in boards .... 75 cts.

Paper covers .... 50 cts.

Dick's Hand-book of Whist. Containing Pole's and Clay's Rules for playing the modern scientific game, the Club Rules of Whist, and two interesting Double Dummy Problems. This is a thorough treatise on the game of Whist. It covers all the points and intricacies which arise in the game; including the acknowledged code of etiquette observed by the players, with Drayson's remarks on Trumps, their use and abuse, and the modern methods of signaling between partners.......................... 25 cts.

Marache's Manual of Chess. Containing a description of the Board and Pieces, Chess Notation, Technical Terms, with diagrams illustrating them, Laws of the Game, Relative Value of Pieces, Preliminary Games for beginners, Fifty Opening of Games, with the best games and copious notes; Twenty Endings of Games, showing easiest way of effecting checkmate; Thirty-six ingenious Diagram Problems, and sixteen curious Chess Stratagems, being one of the best Books for Beginners ever published. By N. Marache. Bound in cloth .... 50 cts.

Dick's Art of Bowling; or, Bowler's Guide. Giving the correct method of playing, keeping the score, and the latest rules which govern the American and German Games, and their most popular variations; including the Regulations adopted in Matches and Tournaments. Fully illustrated.................. 25 cts.

Trumps' New Card Games. Containing the correct method and rules for playing the games of Hearts, Boodle, Newmarket, Five and Nine or Domino Whist, Solo, and Cayenne Whist. Paper covers .... 25 cts.

Robertson's Guide to the Game of Draughts. Embracing all of the twenty-two well-known Openings, with 3340 Variations, including and correcting all that are given in the leading treatises already published, with about 1200 new and original Variations which appear for the first time in this work, forming a thorough and complete digest and analysis of the Game, with corrections and additions up to the present time. The number of moves aggregate nearly 100,000. Match play by Yates, Wyllie, Barker, and others, will be found regularly classified. A change has been made in the trunks generally, and throughout the whole work there appears much that is fresh and original. Cloth, 8vo., 320 pages... $3.00

Anderson's Checkers. Containing complete Instructions and Rules for playing Checkers or Draughts. Illustrated with Diagrams; including all the Standard Games and their Variations, and numerous Problems with their Solutions. By Andrew Anderson. In a certain sense, this is a reprint of Anderson's Celebrated "Second Edition", revised, corrected, and enlarged by Robert M'Culloch; that is, his play when sound is given intact, and where improvements have been shown they have been incorporated, and unsound play eliminated. Cloth........... $1.50

Spayth's American Draught Player; or, The Theory and Practice of the Scientific Game of Checkers. Simplified and Illustrated with Practical Diagrams. Containing upwards of 1700 Games and Positions. By Henry Spayth. Sixth edition, with over three hundred Corrections and Improvements. Containing: The Standard Laws of the Game—Full Instructions—Draught Board Numbered—Names of the Games, and how formed—The "Theory of the Move and its Changes" practically explained and illustrated with Diagrams. Cloth...................... $3.00

Dunne's Draughts Player's Guide and Companion. A Guide to the Student and a Companion for the Advanced Player. By Frank Dunne. A thoroughly practical work, containing Instructions for beginners, Standard Rules, the "Move" and its changes, End Games, Openings, Illustrative Games, including the Wyllie-Bryden Match Games, the Losing Game, and some of the finest Problems of the day, with their Solutions. It includes also the Spanish, Italian, Polish, and Turkish varieties of the game; the entire work being profusely illustrated by Diagrams exhibiting the Problems and the critical positions in the progress of the games. 12mo., cloth.............................. $1.50

Mortimer's Chess Players' Pocket-book. A complete and handy Manual of all the known Openings and Gambits, with a thorough analysis of each, its variations and defense, the more intricate of which are instructively carried out beyond the opening moves. By James Mortimer. The special feature of this work is the manner in which the notation is arranged in tabular form, by which greater perspicuity is gained for study, and so reduces the bulk that it can easily be carried in the pocket for ready reference. This book is emphatically indorsed by all the leading Chess Critics. Cloth, pocket size........................ 50 cts.

Gossip's Chess Players' Text-book. It introduces a preliminary Game, elucidated step by step for the instruction of beginners. It gives a full and extended analysis of all the Openings and Gambits in general use, with illustrative Games analytically explained, and a number of interesting End Games and Strategic positions calculated to afford advanced players a more thorough insight into the intricacies of the game. Bound in cloth. 156 pages.. 75 cts.

Scattergood's Game of Draughts; or, Checkers Simplified and Explained. With practical Diagrams and Illustrations, together with a Checker-board, numbered and printed in red. Containing the Eighteen Standard Games, with over 200 of the best variations selected from various authors, with some never before published. By D. Scattergood. Bound in cloth, with flexible covers.................................. 50 cts.

Spayth's Game of Draughts. By Henry Spayth. This book is designed as a supplement to "The American Draught Player"; but it is complete in itself. It contains lucid instructions for beginners, Laws of the Game, Diagrams, the score of 364 games, together with 34 novel, instructive, and ingenious "critical positions". Cloth.................................. $1.50

Spayth's Draughts; or, Checkers for Beginners. This treatise was written by Henry Spayth, the celebrated player, and is by far the most complete and instructive elementary work on Draughts ever published. It is profusely illustrated with diagrams of ingenious stratagems, curious positions, and perplexing Problems, and contains a great variety of interesting and instructive Games, progressively arranged and clearly explained with notes, so that the learner may easily comprehend them. With the aid of this Manual a beginner may soon become a proficient in the game. Cloth, gilt side...................... 75 cts.

DICK'S ENCYCLOPEDIA

of Practical Receipts and Processes,

CONTAINING 6,422 PRACTICAL RECEIPTS,

Written in a plain and popular manner, and illustrated with explanatory wood-cuts. Being a comprehensive Book of Reference for the Merchant, Manufacturer, Artisan, Amateur and Housekeeper, embracing valuable information in the Arts, Professions, Trades, Manufactures, including Medicine, Pharmacy and Domestic Economy. It is certainly the most useful book of reference for practical information pertaining to the wants of everyday life ever printed. THE SCIENTIFIC AMERICAN says "It is worthy of a place in the library of any home, work-shop, factory or laboratory". Prominent among the immense mass of subjects treated of in the book, are the following:

The Art of Dyeing;
Hard, Soft and Toilet Soaps;
Tanning;
Distillation;
Imitation Liquors;
Wines, Cordials and Bitters;
Cider;
Brewing;
Perfumery; Cologne Water and Perfumed Spirits;
Flavoring Essences, etc.;
Cosmetics;
Hair Dyes and Washes;
Pomades and Perfumed Oils;
Tooth Powders, etc.;
Syrups;
Alcohol and Alcoholmetry;
Petroleum and Kerosene;
Bleaching and Cleaning;
Scouring and Cleansing;
Vinegar;
Sauces, Catsups and Pickles;
Receipts for the Garden;
To Remove Stains, Spots, etc.;
The Extermination of Vermin;
Pyrotechny and Explosives;
Cements, etc.;
Soluble Glass;
Waterproofing;
Artificial Gems;
Inks and Writing Fluids;
Aniline Colors;
Liquid Colors;
Paints and Pigments;
Drying Oils and Dryers;
Painting and Paper-hanging;
Kalsomine and Whitewash;
Oil and Spirit Varnishes;
Varnishing and Polishing;
Lubricators;
Japanning and Lacquering;
Boot and Harness Blacking;
Photography;
Metals and Alloys;
Soldering and Welding;
Amalgams;
Gilding, Silvering, etc.;
Electrotyping, Electroplating, etc;
Medicinal Preparations;
Patent Medicines;
Medical Receipts;
Weights and Measures.

607 pages, royal octavo, cloth..**$5.00**
Sheep..**6.00**

DICK & FITZGERALD, Publishers.

Box 2975. **NEW YORK.**

COOK BOOKS.

Dinner Napkins, and How to Fold Them. Containing plain and systematic directions for arranging and folding Napkins or Serviettes for the Dinner Table, from the simplest forms to the most elaborate and artistic designs. By Georgiana C. Clark. This little work embraces all the favorite designs in general use for transforming a plain Napkin into one of the most attractive and ornamental appendages to an elegantly arranged Dinner-Table. Some of the patterns being expressly intended for combining artistic display with floral decoration, appropriately symbolic of Bridal and other special occasions.
Profusely illustrated...25 cts.

Mrs. Crowen's American Lady's Cookery Book. Giving every variety of information for ordinary and holiday occasions, and containing over 1,200 Original Receipts for Preparing and Cooking Soups and Broths, Fish and Oysters, Clams, Mussels, Crabs and Terrapins, Meats of all kinds, Poultry and Game, Eggs and Cheese, Vegetables and Salads, Sauces of all kinds, fancy Desserts, Puddings and Custards, Pies and Tarts, Bread and Biscuit, Rolls and Cakes, Preserves and Jellies, Pickles and Catsups, Potted Meats, etc., etc. The whole being a complete system of American Cookery. By Mrs. T. J. Crowen.
480 pages, 12 mo., cloth...$1.50

How to Cook and How to Carve. Giving plain and easily understood directions for preparing and cooking, with the greatest economy, every kind of dish, with complete instructions for serving the same. This Book is just the thing for a young Housekeeper. It is worth a dozen of expensive French books. Paper covers..................30 cts.
Bound in boards with cloth back.......................................50 cts.

The American Home Cook Book. Containing several hundred excellent recipes. The whole based on many years' experience of an American Housewife. Illustrated with engravings. All the recipes in this book are written from actual experience in Cooking. Paper...30 cts.
Boards...50 cts.

The Yankee Cook Book. A new system of Cookery. Containing hundreds of excellent recipes from actual experience in Cooking; also, full explanation in the art of Carving. 126 pages, paper covers.30 cts.
Boards...50 cts.

Soyer's Standard Cookery for the People. Embracing an entirely new System of Plain Cookery and Domestic Economy. By Alexis Soyer. The plain and familiar style adopted in describing the details of the various culinary operations, commends itself to the notice of all economical housekeepers, as it affords the best results with the least expenditure. 214 pages, paper.......................................30 cts.
Boards...50 cts.

The American Housewife and Kitchen Directory. This valuable book embraces three hundred and seventy-eight recipes for cooking all sorts of American dishes in the most economical manner.
Paper...30 cts.
Boards...50 cts.

Souillard's Book of Practical Receipts. For the use of Families, Druggists, Perfumers, Confectioners and Dealers in Soaps and Fancy Articles for the Toilet. By F. A. Souillard. Paper......... 25 cts.

Book of Wonders, Mysteries and Disclosures. A complete hand-book of useful information. Giving a large number of Recipes for the manufacture of valuable articles of every-day use, and of great value to manufacturers, storekeepers, druggists, peddlers and families. To which is added Taxidermy and Traps and Trapping. Paper......25 cts.

BOXING AND WRESTLING.

How to Join a Circus. This contains all the information necessary for those who desire to qualify themselves for the Circus or Gymnasium; with hints to Amateurs and advice to Professional performers; affording thorough instruction in all branches of the business. Illustrated. By the celebrated Tony Denier. By carefully following the advice and instruction contained in this book, any person with a moderate degree of perseverance can become proficient in all the startling acts on the horizontal bar, flying trapeze, and other evolutions that challenge the admiration of all who behold them. 104 pages..............25 cts.

Jerry Thomas' Bar Tender's Guide; or How to Mix all kinds of Fancy Drinks. *An entirely new edition; new plates; new drinks.* Containing clear and reliable directions for mixing all the beverages used in the United States. Embracing Punches, Juleps, Cobblers, Cocktails, etc., etc., in endless variety. By Jerry Thomas. This work also contains the best receipts for preparing bottled Punch, bottled Cocktails, Punch Essences, etc., after the most approved methods; also, all the newest Egg Noggs, Fizzes, Slings, Sours, and other Fancy Drinks in endless variety. 16mo, illuminated paper cover..........................50 cts.
16mo, cloth...75 cts.

Dick's Art of Wrestling. A New Hand-Book of thorough instruction in Wrestling, with the accepted Rules to be observed in the different methods of wrestling generally adopted at the present time. Fully illustrated by well-designed engravings, exhibiting all the aggressive and defensive positions necessary for success................25 cts.

Price's Science of Self-Defense. Illustrated with Engravings. This book was written by Ned Price, the celebrated boxer, and is the best work that was ever written upon the subject of Sparring and Wrestling. It contains all the tricks and stratagems resorted to by professional boxers, and the descriptions of the passes, blows and parries are all clearly explained by the aid of numerous diagrams and engravings. That portion of the work which treats on wrestling is particularly thorough, and is well illustrated with engravings. Boards...............................75 cts.

Ned Donnelly's Art of Boxing. A thorough Manual of Sparring and Self-Defence, illustrated with Forty Engravings, showing the various Blows, Stops and Guards; by Ned Donnelly, Professor of Boxing to the London Athletic Club, etc., etc. This work explains in detail every movement of attack and defence in the clearest language, and in accordance with the most approved and modern methods; the engravings are very distinctly drawn, and show each position and motion as plainly as the personal instruction of a professor could convey it. It teaches all the feints and dodges practised by experienced boxers, and gives advice to those who desire to perfect themselves in the Manly Art. Including the London Prize Ring Rules, and revised Marquis of Queensbury's Rules. 127 pages...25 cts.

The Art of Attack and Defence. A Manual of Fencing, Sword Exercise, Bayonet Practice and Boxing, affording instructions in the modern method of Fencing, the mode of attack with sword against sword or bayonet, and with bayonet against sword or bayonet. By Major W. J. Elliott. Profusely illustrated.....................................25 cts.

Boxing Made Easy; or, The Complete Manual of Self-Defense. Clearly explained and Illustrated in a Series of Easy Lessons, with some important Hints to Wrestlers...............................15 cts.

RECITATIONS AND DIALOGUES.

Dick's Series of Recitations and Readings. Nos. 1 to 16.
Dick's Dutch, French and Yankee Recitations.
Dick's Irish Recitations.
Dick's Comic and Dialect Recitations.
Dick's Diverting Dialogues.
Dick's Dialogues and Monologues.
Dick's Comic Dialogues.
McBride's Funny Dialogues.
McBride's Comic Dialogues.
McBride's All Kinds of Dialogues.
McBride's New Dialogues.
McBride's Humorous Dialogues.
McBride's Temperance Dialogues.
McBride's Comic Speeches and Recitations.
Frost's Dialogues for Young Folks.
Frost's Humorous and Exhibition Dialogues.
Frost's New Dialogues.
Kavanaugh's Comic Pieces for Very Little Children.
Kavanaugh's Humorous Dramas.
Kavanaugh's Juvenile Speaker, for Very Little Children.
Kavanaugh's Exhibition Reciter, for Very Little Children.
Kavanaugh's New Speeches and Dialogues.
Holmes' Very Little Dialogues for Very Little Folks.
Graham's School Dialogues for Young People.
Steele's Exhibition Dialogues.
Martine's Droll Dialogues and Laughable Recitations.
Beecher's Recitations and Readings.
Howard's Recitations; Comic, Serious and Pathetic.
Wilson's Recitations for School Declamation.
Spencer's Comic Speeches and Recitations.
Barton's Comic Recitations and Dialogues.

The price of each of the above books in paper covers is 30 cents; or bound in boards, with cloth back, 50 cents; sent by mail, postage paid, to any address on receipt of the price.

Send for catalogue, mailed free, giving full contents of each book, and the number and sex of the characters required for the dialogues.

MODEL SPEECHES AND SKELETON ESSAYS.

Ogden's Model Speeches for all School Occasions. Containing Original Addresses and Orations on everything appertaining to School Life: comprising Set Speeches on all occasions connected with Schools, Academies and Colleges, for School Officers, as well as for Teachers and Students of both sexes, with appropriate replies. By Christol Ogden.

This original work contains over one-hundred telling speeches and replies in well-chosen words, and every variety of style, for

All Kinds of School Ceremonials.
Speeches on Opening and Dedicating New Schools and Academies.
Salutatory and Valedictory Addresses.
Presentations and Conferring Honors.
Burlesque Speeches.
Addresses to Teachers.
Prologues and Epilogues for School Exhibitions
Anniversary Congratulations.

Including practical hints on Extempore speaking with a dissertation on the selection of appropriate topics, suitable style, and effective delivery, and also valuable advice to those who lack confidence when addressing the Public. Paper... ....50 cts.
Bound in boards...75 cts.

Ogden's Skeleton Essays; or Authorship in Outline. Consisting of Condensed Treatises on popular subjects, with references to sources of information, and directions how to enlarge them into Essays, or expand them into Lectures. Fully elucidated by example as well as precept. By Christol Ogden.

In this work is a thorough analysis of some SEVENTY prominent and popular subjects, with extended specimens of the method of enlarging them into Essays and Lectures.

The following interesting topics are separately and ably argued on both sides of the question, thus presenting also well digested matter for Debate, being on subjects of absorbing interest everywhere:—

Bi-Metalism.
Civil Service Reform.
Prohibition.
Is Marriage a Failure?
City and Country.
The Credit System.
Free Trade and Protection.
Capital Punishment.
Shall More or Less be Taught in Public Schools.

All the remaining subjects are equally thoroughly discussed, and form a valuable aid to the student in preparing compositions, essays, etc.
Paper...50 cts.
Bound in boards...75 cts.

Dick's Book of Toasts, Speeches and Responses. Containing Toasts and Sentiments for Public and Social Occasions, and specimen Speeches with appropriate replies suitable for the following occasions:

Public Dinners.
Social Dinners.
Convivial Gatherings.
Art and Professional Banquets.
Agricultural and Commercial Festivals.
Special Toasts for Ladies.
Christmas, Thanksgiving and other Festivals.
Friendly Meetings.
Weddings and their Anniversaries.
Army and Navy Banquets.
Patriotic and Political Occasions.
Trades' Unions and Dinners.
Benedicts' and Bachelors' Banquets.
Masonic Celebrations.
All Kinds of Occasions.

This work includes an instructive dissertation on the Art of making amusing After-dinner Speeches, giving hints and directions by the aid of which persons with only ordinary intelligence can make an entertaining and telling speech. Also, Correct Rules and Advice for Presiding at Table.

The use of this work will render a poor and diffident speaker fluent and witty—and a good speaker better and wittier besides affording an immense fund of anecdotes, wit and wisdom, and other serviceable matter to draw upon at will. Paper.......................................30 cts.
Bound in boards...50 cts.

DEBATES AND READY MADE SPEECHES.

Barber's American Book of Ready-Made Speeches. Containing 159 original examples of Humorous and Serious Speeches, suitable for every possible occasion where a speech may be called for, together with appropriate replies to each. Including:

Presentation Speeches,
Convivial Speeches.
Festival Speeches.
Addresses of Congratulation.
Addresses of Welcome.
Addresses of Compliment.
Political Speeches.
Dinner and Supper Speeches for Clubs.
Off-Hand Speeches on a Variety of Subjects.
Miscellaneous Speeches.
Toasts and Sentiments for Public and Private Entertainments.
Preambles and Resolutions of Congratulation, Compliment and Condolence.

With this book any person may prepare himself to make a neat little speech, or reply to one when called upon to do so. They are all short, appropriate and witty, and even ready speakers may profit by them. Paper..**50 cts.**
Bound in boards, cloth backs....................................**75 cts.**

How to Conduct a Debate. A Series of Complete Debates, Outlines of Debates and Questions for Discussion. In the complete debates, the questions for discussion are defined, the debate formally opened, an array of brilliant arguments adduced on either side, and the debate closed according to parliamentary usages. The second part consists of questions for debate, with heads of arguments, for and against, given in a condensed form, for the speakers to enlarge upon to suit their own fancy. In addition to these is a large collection of debatable questions. The authorities to be referred to for information are given at the close of every debate throughout the work. By F. Rowton. 232 pages.
Paper covers..**50 cts.**
Bound in boards, cloth back..................................**75 cts.**

The Debater, Chairman's Assistant, and Rules of Order. A manual for Instruction and Reference in all matters pertaining to the Management of Public Meetings according to Parliamentary usages. It gives all necessary details connected with the following topics:—

How to Form and Conduct all kinds of Associations and Clubs:
How to Organize and arrange Public Meetings, Celebrations, Dinners, Picnics and Conventions;
Forms for Constitutions of Lyceums or Institutes, Literary and other Societies;
The Powers and Duties of Officers, with Forms for Treasurers', Secretaries', and other regular or occasional Official Reports;
The Formation and Duties of Committees;
Rules of Order, and Order of Business, with Mode of Procedure in all cases. Also the Rules of Order in Tabular Form for instant reference in all Cases of Doubt that may arise, enabling a Chairman to decide on all points at a glance;
How to draft Resolutions, Reports and Petitions on various subjects and for various occasions, with numerous model examples;
A Model Debate, introducing the greatest possible variety of points of order, with correct Decisions by the Chairman;

This work includes all Decisions and Rulings up to the present day.
Paper covers..**30 cts.**
Bound in Boards, cloth back..................................**50 cts.**

How to Learn the Sense of 3,000 French Words in one Hour. It is a fact that there are at least three thousand words in the French language, forming a large proportion of those used in ordinary conversation, which are spelled the same as in English...........**25 cts.**

500 French Phrases, with their English Translations. The phrases here given are all selected for their general usefulness for occasional quotation...**10 cts.**

COMPOSITION AND LANGUAGES.

Live and Learn; or, One Thousand Mistakes of Daily Occurrence in Speaking, Writing and Pronunciation, Corrected and Explained. There are hundreds of persons who are sensible of their deficiencies on many points connected with the Grammar of their own tongue, and who, by self-tuition, may correct such deficiencies.

It Corrects and Explains 1,000 Mistakes of Daily Occurrence in Speaking, Writing and Pronunciation.
It Explains the many Perplexing points that occasion difficulty to the student.
It explains most of the Latin and French words and phrases of frequent occurrence in newspapers.
It shows how to punctuate and paragraph correctly.
It shows all the current improprieties of expression and gives rules for their correction.
It gives clear rules for the use of Capitals and Italics.
It gives plain, general rules for spelling.
It gives detailed instructions for writing for the Press in the various departments of newspaper and general literature.

213 pages, paper..30 cts.
Bound in boards..50 cts.

Walker's Rhyming, Spelling and Pronouncing Dictionary of the English Language. To which is added critical and practical Observations on Orthography, Syllabication, Pronunciation, an Index of Allowable Rhymes, with Authorities for their usage, etc.
Royal 12mo, 700 pages..$3.00

How to Write a Composition. The use of this book will save the student the many hours of labor too often wasted in trying to write a plain composition. It affords a perfect skeleton of one hundred and seventeen different subjects, with their divisions clearly defined, and each heading filled in with the ideas which the subject suggests; so that all the writer has to do, in order to produce a good composition is to enlarge on them to suit his taste. 178 pages, paper..................30 cts.
Bound in boards..50 cts.

The Poet's Companion. A Dictionary of all Allowable Rhymes in the English Language. This gives the Perfect, the Imperfect and Allowable Rhymes, and will enable you to ascertain to a certainty whether any word can be mated. It is invaluable to any one who desires to court the Muses, and is used by some of the best writers......25 cts.

Mind Your Stops. Punctuation made plain, and Composition simplified for Readers, Writers and talkers.......................12 cts.

Thimm's French Self-Taught. A new system on the most simple principles, for universal Self-Tuition, with English pronunciation of every word. By this system the acquirement of the French Language is rendered less laborious and more thorough than by any of the old methods. By Franz Thimm....................................25 cts.

Thimm's German Self-Taught. Uniform with "French Self-Taught," and arranged in accordance with the same principles of thoroughness and simplicity. By Franz Thimm....................25 cts.

Thimm's Spanish Self-Taught. A book of self-instruction in the Spanish Language, arranged according to the same method as the "French" and "German," by the same author, and uniform with them in size. By Franz Thimm....................................25 cts.

Thimm's Italian Self-Taught. Uniform in style and size with the three foregoing books. By Franz Thimm...............25 cts.

LETTER WRITERS.

Martine's Sensible Letter-Writer. Being a comprehensive and complete Guide and Assistant for those who desire to carry on Epistolary Correspondence; containing a large collection of model letters on the simplest matters of life, adapted to all ages, conditions and occasions,

EMBRACING,

Business Letters;
Applications for Employment, with Letters of Recommendation and Answers to Advertisements;
Letters between Parents and Children;
Letters of Friendly Counsel;
Letters soliciting Advice, Assistance and Friendly Favors;
Letters of Courtesy, Friendship and Affection;
Letters of Condolence and Sympathy;
A Choice Collection of Love Letters, for Every Situation in a Courtship;
Notes of Ceremony, Familiar Invitations, etc., together with Notes of Acceptance and Regret.

The whole containing 300 Sensible Letters and Notes. This is an invaluable book for those persons who have not had sufficient practice to enable them to write letters without great effort. It contains such a variety of letters that models may be found to suit every subject.
207 pages, bound in boards, cloth back........................**50 cts.**
Bound in cloth, cloth back..**75 cts.**

Frost's Original Letter-Writer. A complete collection of Original Letters and Notes upon every imaginable subject of Every-Day Life, with plain directions about everything connected with writing a letter. By S. A. Frost. To which is added a comprehensive Table of Synonyms, alone worth double the price asked for the book. We assure our readers that it is the best collection of letters ever published in this country; they are written in plain and natural language, and elegant in style without being high-flown. Bound in boards, cloth back..............**50 cts.**

North's Book of Love-Letters. With directions how to write and when to use them, and 120 Specimen Letters, suitable for Lovers of any age and condition, and under all circumstances, with the author's comments thereon. Being a Hand-book of valuable information and counsel for the use of those who need friendly guidance and advice in matters of Love, Courtship and Marriage. By Ingoldsby North.
Boards..**50 cts.**
Bound in cloth..**75 cts.**

Worcester's Letter-Writer and Book of Business Forms for Ladies and Gentlemen. Containing Accurate Directions for Conducting Epistolary Correspondence, with 270 Specimen Letters, adapted to every Age and Situation in Life, and to Business Pursuits in General; with an Appendix comprising Forms for Wills, Petitions, Bills, Receipts, Drafts, Bills of Exchange, Promissory Notes, Executors' and Administrators' Accounts, etc., etc. The Orthography of the entire work is based on Worcester's method, which is coming more and more into general use.
This work is divided into two parts, the portion for Ladies being kept distinct from the rest of the book, in order to provide better facilities for ready reference. 216 pages, boards, cloth back..................**50 cts.**

Frost's Twenty-Five Cent Letter-Writer. Containing Three Hundred Letters and appropriate Replies upon every subject of daily life, including plain Directions on all the details which constitute a well-written Letter. It would be difficult to find any want or occasion in life which requires correspondence that is not fairly supplied by some letter or letters in this comprehensive collection, affording just what is needed or an excellent model which can be easily modified to suit the most peculiar circumstances. Paper...........................**25 cts.**

LETTER WRITERS.

Dick's Common Sense Letter Writer. Containing Three Hundred and Sixty Sensible Social and Business Letters with appropriate Answers on the following subjects:

Letters of Introduction.
Soliciting and Granting Favors.
Accompanying Gifts.
Acknowledging Gifts and Favors.
Letters of Congratulation.
Letters of Sympathy and Condolence.
Answers to Advertisements for Help Wanted.
Inquiries about and Recommendations of Character and Ability.
Letters between Employers and Employed.
Accepting and Resigning Positions.
Letters of Apology.
Letters of Remonstrance and Complaint.
Letters of Love and Courtship.
Letters of Invitation and Acceptance.
Forms of Cards of Invitation.
Notes of Postponement.
Notes Offering Escort.
Letters to Landlords and about Board and Apartments.
Family Letters on Various Subjects.
Business Correspondence.
Letters on Miscellaneous Subjects.

Including Instructions for the arrangement of the different parts of a Letter, the Address, &c. By William B. Dick. The Letters are all original, and serve as eminent models of matter, expression and style, in plain but well-chosen language and clearness of diction; the great variety of letters on each subject offers a wide field for choice, and with, perhaps, a little modification could be made available for every possible contingency. Bound in boards.....................................**50 cts.**

Dick's Commercial Letter Writer, and Book of Business Forms. Containing entirely original Models of Letters on all business subjects, with appropriate replies; also, several specimens of continuous Correspondence, exhibiting by a series of Letters, the commencement, progress, and completion of Mercantile Transactions. By WILLIAM B. DICK.
This work includes correct forms for Business Notices and Cards, and Partnership Announcements; for Applications for Employment and neatly-worded Answers to Inquiries and Advertisements; for occasional Circulars, properly displayed, and for drawing up Business Documents, Notes, Checks, Receipts, Mortgages, Assignments, Wills, Power of Attorney, Letters of Credit, Account-Sales, Accounts Current, Invoices, Bills of Lading, &c., and the correct method of adjusting General and Particular Averages.
It contains, in addition, a Glossary of Technical Terms used in Commerce; a rapid and simple method of computing Interest; a Table showing the value of Foreign Coins in United States' Currency; and other useful, practical and interesting information, in all the details necessary for conducting commercial correspondence. 200 pages, boards..................**50 cts.**

Dick's Letter Writer for Ladies. Consisting of over Five Hundred entirely original Letters and Notes, with various replies, on every subject and occasion that a Lady in good society could possibly require. They are all new and written expressly for this work.
These letters, &c., are excellent models of ease and elegant style, facility in method of expression, and correct form; they furnish, therefore, valuable aid to Ladies, who, however otherwise accomplished, are deficient in the necessary acquirement of the graceful and properly-worded correspondence which their social position demands. 268 pages, boards.....**50 cts.**

Chesterfield's Letter-Writer and Complete Book of Etiquette. Containing the Art of Letter-Writing simplified, a guide to friendly, affectionate, polite and business correspondence, and rules for punctuation and spelling, with complete rules of Etiquette and the usages of Society. An excellent hand-book for reference.
Bound in boards...**40 cts.**

CHECKERS OR DRAUGHTS.

Robertson's Guide to the Game of Draughts. Embracing all of the twenty-two well-known Openings, with 3,340 Variations, including and correcting all that are given in the leading treatises already published, with about 1,200 new and original Variations which appear for the first time in this work, forming a thorough and complete digest and analysis of the Game with corrections and additions up to the present time. The number of moves aggregate nearly 100,000. Match play by Yates, Wylie, Barker and others, will be found regularly classified. A change has been made in the trunks generally, and throughout the whole work there appears much that is fresh and original, instead of the usual well-worn book play. Bound in cloth, 8vo, 320 pages........**$3.00**

Anderson's Checkers. Containing complete Instructions and rules for playing Checkers or Draughts. Illustrated with Diagrams; including all the Standard Games and their Variations, and numerous Problems with their Solutions. By Andrew Anderson. In a certain sense, this is a reprint of Anderson's Celebrated "Second Edition", revised, corrected and enlarged by Robert M'Culloch; that is, his play when sound is given intact, and where improvements have been shown they have been incorporated, and unsound play eliminated.
12mo, cloth **$1.50**

Spayth's American Draught Player; or the Theory and Practice of the Scientific Game of Checkers. Simplified and Illustrated with Practical Diagrams. Containing upwards of 1,700 Games and Positions. By Henry Spayth. Sixth edition with over three hundred Corrections and Improvements. Containing: The Standard Laws of the Game—Full instructions—Draught Board Numbered—Names of the Games, and how formed—The "Theory of the Move and its Changes" practically explained and illustrated with Diagrams—Playing Tables for Draught Clubs—New Systems of Numbering the Board—Prefixing signs to the Variations—List of Draught Treatises and Publications chronologically arranged. Bound in cloth, giltside and back......**$3.00**

Spayth's Game of Draughts. By Henry Spayth. This book is designed as a supplement to the author's first work, "The American Draught Player"; but it is complete in itself. It contains lucid instructions for beginners, laws of the game, diagrams, the score of 364 games, together with 34 novel, instructive and ingenious "critical positions". Cloth, gilt back and side...**$1.50**

Spayth's Draughts or Checkers for Beginners. This treatise was written by Henry Spayth, the celebrated player, and is by far the most complete and instructive elementary work on Draughts ever published. It is profusely illustrated with diagrams of ingenious stratagems, curious positions and perplexing Problems and contains a great variety of interesting and instructive Games, progressively arranged and clearly explained with notes, so that the learner may easily comprehend them. With the aid of this Manual a beginner may soon become a proficient in the game. Cloth, gilt side...........................**75 cts.**

Scattergood's Game of Draughts, or Checkers Simplified and Explained. With practical Diagrams and Illustrations, together with a Checker-Board, numbered and printed in red. Containing the Eighteen Standard Games, with over 200 of the best variations selected from various authors. with some never before published. By D. Scattergood. Bound in cloth, with flexible covers......................**50 cts.**

CHESS AND CARD GAMES.

Mortimer's Chess Players' Pocket-Book. A complete and handy Manual of all the known Openings and Gambits, with a thorough analysis of each, its variations and defense, the more intricate of which are instructively carried out beyond the opening moves. By James Mortimer. The special feature of this work is the manner in which the notation is arranged in tabular form, by which greater perspicuity is gained for study, and so reduces the bulk that it can easily be carried in the pocket for ready reference. This book is emphatically endorsed by all the leading Chess Critics. Cloth, pocket size..................50 cts.

Gossip's Chess-Players' Text Book. It introduces a preliminary Game, elucidated step by step for the instruction of beginners. It gives a full and extended analysis of all the Openings and Gambits in general use, with illustrative Games analytically explained, and a number of interesting End-Games and Strategic positions calculated to afford advanced players a more thorough insight into the intricacies of the Game. Bound in Cloth. 156 pages..........................75 cts.

Marache's Manual of Chess. Containing a description of the Board and Pieces, Chess Notation, Technical Terms, with diagrams illustrating them, Laws of the Game, Relative Value of Pieces, Preliminary Games for beginners, Fifty Openings of Games, giving all the latest discoveries of Modern Masters, with the best games and copious notes; Twenty Endings of Games, showing easiest way of effecting checkmate; Thirty-six ingenious Diagram Problems, and sixteen curious Chess Stratagems, being one of the best Books for Beginners ever published. By N. Marache. Bound in cloth, gilt side..............................50 cts.

Dick's Hand-Book of Cribbage. Containing full directions for playing all the Varieties of the Game. and the Laws which govern them. This work is ENTIRELY NEW, and gives the correct method of playing the Six-Card, Five-Card, Two-Handed, Three-Handed, and Four-Handed Varieties of the Game, with instructive examples, showing clearly all the combinations of Hand, Crib, and Play, with a thorough investigation of long sequences in play, and the value of Hands. The Laws of the game have been carefully revised in accordance with the recognized usages of the present time, and constitute a reliable authority on all points of the Game. 18mo., cloth, flexible.....................................50 cts.

Dick's Hand-Book of Whist. Containing Pole's and Clay's Rules for playing the modern scientific game, the Club Rules of Whist, and two interesting Double Dummy Problems. This is a thorough treatise on the game of Whist, taken from "The American Hoyle" which is the standard authority. It covers all the points and intricacies which arise in the game; including the acknowledged code of etiquette observed by the players, with Drayson's remarks on Trumps, their use and abuse, and all the modern methods of signalling between partners.............25 cts.

Pole on Whist: The Theory of the Modern Scientific Game of Whist. By William Pole, F. R. S. This complete and exhaustive Treatise on the Game is in handy form for the pocket, and affords lucid instructions at all stages of the game for partners to play in combination for their best interests. 14th Edition.............................20 cts.

The Game of Euchre. Containing the Game tersely described, valuable hints and advice to learners, the latest rules, and all necessary directions for playing the Two-Handed, Three-Handed (or Cut-Throat) and Four-Handed Games, clearly explained. Vest pocket size....15 cts.

Dick's Original Album Verses and Acrostics. Containing a voluminous and varied collection of Original Verses written expressly

For Autograph Albums;	*For Album Dedications;*
To Accompany Bouquets;	*To Accompany Philopena Forfeits;*
For Birthday Anniversaries;	*For Congratulation;*
For Wooden, Tin, Crystal, Silver and Golden Weddings;	*For Valentines in General and all Trades and Professions.*

It contains also Two Hundred and Eighteen Original Acrostic Verses, the initial letters of each verse forming a different Lady's Christian name, the meaning and derivation of the name being appended to each. The primary object of this book is to furnish entirely fresh and unhackneyed matter for all who may be called upon to fill and adorn a page in a Lady's Album; but it contains also new and appropriate verses to suit Birthday, Wedding, and all other Anniversaries and Occasions to which verses of Compliment or Congratulation are applicable. Paper covers..........50 cts. Bound in full cloth..75 cts.

Sut Lovingood. Yarns spun by a "Nat'ral Born Durn'd Fool", Warped and Wove for Public Wear, by George W. Harris. Illustrated with eight fine full page engravings, from designs by Howard. It would be difficult, we think, to cram a larger amount of pungent humor into 300 pages than will be found in this really funny book. The Preface and Dedication are models of sly simplicity, and the 24 Sketches which follow are among the best specimens of broad burlesque to which the genius of the ludicrous, for which the Southwest is so distinguished, has yet given birth. 12mo., cloth..$1.50

Dick's Mysteries of the Hand; or, Palmistry made Easy. Translated, Abridged and Arranged from the French Works of Desbarrolles, D'Arpentigny and De Para d'Hermes. The various lines and mounts on the palm of the hand, and the typical formation of the hand and fingers are all clearly explained and illustrated by diagrams. The meaning to be deduced from the greater or less development of these mounts and lines (each of which has its own signification), also from the length, thickness and shape of the thumb and fingers, and from the mutual bearing they exercise on each other, is all distinctly explained. Complete facility for instant reference is insured by means of marginal notes by which any point of detail may be found and consulted at a glance. By means of this book the hitherto occult mystery of Palmistry is made simple and easy, and the whole Art may be acquired without difficulty or delay. It is emphatically Palmistry in a nutshell, and by its use, character and disposition can be discerned and probable future destiny foretold with surprising accuracy. Illuminated paper cover......................50 cts.

Lola Montez' Arts of Beauty; or, Secrets of a Lady's Toilet. *With Hints to Gentlemen on the Art of Fascinating.* Lola Montez here explains all the Arts employed by the celebrated beauties and ladies in Paris and other cities of Europe, for the purpose of preserving their beauty and improving and developing their charms. The recipes are all clearly given, so that any person can understand them. Paper....25 cts.

Lander's Revised Work of Odd-Fellowship. Containing all the Lectures, complete, with Regulations for Opening, Conducting, and Closing a Lodge; together with forms of Initiation, Charges of the Various Officers, etc., with the Complete work in the following degrees: Initiation; First, or Pink Degree; Second, or Royal Blue Degree; Third, or Scarlet Degree. By EDWIN F. LANDER. This hand-book of the Revised Work of the Independent Order of Odd-Fellowship has been prepared in conformity with the amendments and alterations adopted by the Sovereign Grand Lodge of Canada, September, 1880. 16mo, paper cover...25 cts.

READY RECKONERS AND LUMBER MEASURERS.

Day's American Ready-Reckoner. This Ready-Reckoner is composed of Original Tables, which are positively correct, having been revised in the most careful manner. It is a book of 192 pages, and embraces more matter than 500 pages of any other Reckoner. It contains: Tables for Rapid Calculations of Aggregate Values, Wages, Salaries, Board, Interest Money, etc.; Tables of Timber and Plank Measurement; Tables of Board and Log Measurement, and a great variety of Tables and useful calculations which it would be impossible to enumerate in an advertisement of this limited space. All the information in this valuable book is given in a simple manner, and is made so plain, that any person can use it at once without any previous study or loss of time.
Boards..50 cts.
Cloth..75 cts.

Brisbane's Golden Ready-Reckoner. Calculated in Dollars and Cents. Showing at once the amount or value of any number of articles or quantity of goods, or any merchandise, either by gallon, quart, pint, ounce, pound, quarter hundred, yard, foot, inch, bushel, etc., in an easy and plain manner. Boards..............................35 cts.

Dick's Log and Lumber Measurer. A complete set of Tables, with full instructions for their use, showing at a glance the cubical contents of logs and the feet of inch-boards they contain by Doyle's Rule, the measurement of timber of all kinds and dimensions, and all other necessary information for measuring and estimating the value of lumber according to present usages. It includes also useful and practical Tables of Wages by the day, week, and month, and valuable statistical matter of interest to carpenters, builders, and the lumber trade. All the tables are new, reliable, and proved correct. Boards........................25 cts.

Row's Complete Fractional Ready Reckoner. For buying and selling any kind of merchandise, giving the fractional parts of a pound, yard, etc., from one-quarter to one thousand at any price from one-quarter of a cent to five dollars. 36mo, 232 pages. Boards....50 cts.

Row's National Wages Tables. Showing at a glance the amount of wages, from half an hour to sixty hours, at from $1 to $37 per week. Also from one-quarter of a day to four weeks, at $1 to $37 per week. By this book a large pay-roll can be made out in a few minutes, thus saving more time in making out one pay-roll than the cost of the book. 80 pages, half bound.................................50 cts.

The Magicians Own Book; or, The Whole Art of Conjuring. A complete hand-book of Parlor Magic, containing over a thousand Optical, Chemical, Mechanical, Magnetic and Magical Experiments, Astonishing Sleights and Subtleties, Celebrated Card Deceptions, Ingenious Tricks with Numbers, curious and entertaining Puzzles, the art of Secret Writing, together with all the most noted tricks of modern performers. Illustrated with over 500 wood-cuts, 12mo, cloth, gilt..............$1.50

The American Boy's Manual of Practical Mechanics. Prominent among the wide range of subjects embraced in this book are Carpentry and Carpenters' Tools; Plain and Ornamental Turning in Woods, Metal, etc.; the construction of various model Steam Engines and Steamboats; Boat and Canoe building, Telegraphy, and the various batteries employed; Electrotyping, Dioramas, Sand Clocks, Glass Blowing and Gilding on Glass; Magic Lanterns, and Calcium Lights; Aquaria; Telescopes; Balloons, and Fireworks; and other useful and ornamental appliances. Profusely illustrated. 169 pages, 8vo, paper..........50 cts.
Bound in cloth..$1.00

HUMOROUS BOOKS.

Dr. Valentine's Comic Lectures; or, Morsels of Mirth for the Melancholy. Containing Comic Lectures on Heads, Faces, Noses and Mouths; Comic Lectures on Animal Magnetism; Burlesque Specimens of Stump Eloquence; Transactions of Learned Societies; Comical Delineation of Eccentric Characters; Amusing Colloquies and Monologues. With twelve portraits of Dr. Valentine in character......**30 cts.**

Mrs. Partington's Carpet-Bag of Fun. Containing the Queer Sayings of Mrs. Partington, and the Funny Doings of her remarkable Son Isaac. Also the most amusing collection extant of Playful Puns, Phunny Poems, Pleasing Prose, Popular Parodies, and Political Pasquinades, Rhymes Without Reason and Reason Without Rhymes, Anecdotes, Conundrums, Anagrams, etc. Illustrated. Paper...............**30 cts.**

Yale College Scrapes; or, How the Boys Go it at New Haven. This is a book of 114 pages, containing accounts of all the famous "Scrapes" and "Sprees" of which students of Old Yale have been guilty for the last quarter of a century.................................**25 cts.**

Chips From Uncle Sam's Jack-Knife. Illustrated with over 100 Comical Engravings, and comprising a collection of over 500 Laughable Stories, Funny Adventures, Comic Poetry, Queer Conundrums, Terrific Puns and Sentimental Sentences..........................**25 cts.**

Fox's Ethiopian Comicalities. Containing Strange Sayings, Eccentric Doings, Burlesque Speeches, Laughable Drolleries and Funny Stories, by the celebrated Ethiopian Comedian Charles Fox.......**10 cts.**

Ned Turner's Circus Joke Book. A collection of the best Jokes, Bon Mots, Repartees, Gems of Wit and Funny Sayings and Doings of the celebrated Equestrian Clown and Ethiopian Comedian, Ned Turner..**10 cts.**

Ned Turner's Black Jokes. A collection of Funny Stories, Jokes and Conundrums, with Witty Sayings and Humorous Dialogues, as given by Ned Turner..**10 cts.**

Ned Turner's Clown Joke Book. Containing the best Jokes and Gems of Wit, composed and delivered by Ned Turner.........**10 cts.**

Charley White's Joke Book. Containing a full exposé of all the most Laughable Jokes, Witticisms, etc., as told by the celebrated Ethiopian Comedian, Charles White.............................**10 cts.**

Black Wit and Darky Conversations. Containing laughable Anecdotes, Jokes and Darky Conversations.................**10 cts.**

Broad Grins of the Laughing Philosopher. This book is full of the drollest and queerest incidents imaginable, interspersed with jokes, quaint sayings and funny pictures.... ....**13 cts.**

Very, Very Funny. Containing the Cream of the best funny things published in "Puck", "The Detroit Free Press," "Norristown Herald," "Peck's Sun," "Texas Siftings," "Arkansaw Traveler," etc. No threadbare jokes, but everything fresh and profusely illustrated, **10cts.**

How to Speak in Public; or, the Art of Extempore Oratory. A valuable manual for those who desire to become ready off-hand speakers; containing clear directions how to arrange ideas logically and quickly, including examples of speeches delivered by some of the greatest orators. Paper...**25 cts.**

HUMOROUS BOOKS.

Jack Johnson's Jokes for the Jolly. A collection of Funny Stories, Droll Incidents, Queer Conceits and Apt Repartees. Illustrating the Drolleries of Border Life in the West, Yankee Peculiarities, Dutch Blunders, French Sarcasms, Irish Wit and Humor, etc., with short Ludicrous Narratives. Paper..25 cts.

Snipsnaps and Snickerings of Simon Snodgrass. A collection of Laughable Irish Stories, Dutch Blunders, Yankee Tricks and Dodges, Backwoods Boasting, Humors of Horse-trading, Negro Comicalities, Frenchmen's Queer Mistakes, Scotch Shrewdness, and other phases of eccentric character. It is also full of funny engravings.......25 cts.

The Strange and Wonderful Adventures of Bachelor Butterfly. Showing how his passion for Natural history completely eradicated the tender passion implanted in his breast—also detailing his Extraordinary Travels both by sea and land—his Hair-breadth Escapes from fire and cold—his being come over by a Widow with nine small children—and other Perils of a most extraordinary nature. The whole illustrated by about 200 engravings..............................30 cts.

The Laughable Adventures of Messrs. Brown, Jones, and Robinson. Showing where they went, and how they went, what they did and how they did it. Here is a book which will make you split your sides laughing. It shows the comical adventures of three jolly young greenhorns, who went travelling, and got into all manner of scrapes and funny adventures. Illustrated with nearly 200 comic engravings......30 cts.

The Jolly Joker; or, a Laugh all Round. An Immense Collection of the Funniest Jokes, Drollest Anecdotes and most Side-Splitting Oddities in existence. The illustrations alone are sufficient for a constant and long-sustained series of good square laughs for all time.
12 mo, 144 pages. Paper..25 cts.

The Mishaps and Adventures of Obadiah Oldbuck. This humorous and curious book sets forth, with 188 comic drawings, the misfortunes which befell Mr. Oldbuck; and also his five unsuccessful attempts to commit suicide—his hair-breadth escapes from fire, water and famine—his affection for his poor dog, etc. To look over this book will make you laugh, and you can't help it.......................30 cts.

Uncle Josh's Trunkful of Fun. Containing a rich collection of

Comical Stories, Cruel Sells,
Side-Splitting Jokes, Humorous Poetical Drolleries,
Quaint Parodies, Burlesque Sermons.
New Conundrums, Mirth-Provoking Speeches.
Curious Puzzles, Amusing Card Tricks, and
Astonishing Feats of Parlor-Magic.

This book is illustrated with nearly 200 funny engravings, and contains, in 64 large octavo double-column pages, at least three times as much reading matter and real fun as any other book of the price.......15 cts.

Draiper's Six Hundred Ways to Make Money. A reliable Compendium of valuable Receipts for making articles in constant demand and of ready sale, carefully selected from private sources and the best established authorities. By Edmund S. Draiper, Professor of Analytical Chemistry, etc. This Collection of Receipts is undoubtedly the most valuable and comprehensive that has ever been offered to the public in so cheap a form. 144 pages, paper..........................30 cts.

The Life, Crime and Capture of John Wilkes Booth. With a full Sketch of the Conspiracy of which he was the Leader, and the Pursuit, Trial and Execution of his Accomplices. By George Alfred Townsend. Illustrated on the cover with a fine portrait of the Assassin, and also containing Plans, Maps, etc..................................25 cts.

THEATRICALS, DIALOGUES AND TABLEAUX.

Weldon's Fancy Costumes. Containing complete instructions how to make an immense variety of Historical, National and Fancy Dresses; giving minute details regarding the color and quantity of all the materials needed for each Costume, and illustrated with over fifty full-page engravings..50 cts.

Tony Denier's Parlor Tableaux, or Living Pictures. Containing about eighty popular subjects, with plain directions for arranging the stage, dressing-room, lights, full description of costumes, duties of stage manager, properties and scenery required, and all the directions for getting them up. Among the contents there are nine tableaux for *male* and an equal number for *female* characters only. Everything is stated in a plain, simple manner, so that it will be easily understood; everything like style or unnecessary show has been avoided. Price..........25 cts.

Tony Denier's Secret of Performing Shadow Pantomimes. Showing how to get them up and how to act in them; with full and concise instructions and numerous illustrations. Also full and complete descriptions of properties and costumes. Price... ....25 cts.

Pollard's Artistic Tableaux. With Picturesque Diagrams and descriptions of Costumes. Text by Josephine Pollard; arrangement of Diagrams by Walter Satterlee. This excellent work gives all the necessary information in relation to the preparation of the stage, the dressing and grouping of the characters. and the method of arranging everything so as to produce the proper effects. It is furnished with descriptive diagrams by an artist who has had large experience in the arrangement of tableaux. Paper..30 cts.

Frost's Book of Tableaux and Shadow Pantomimes. A collection of Tableaux Vivants and Shadow Pantomimes, with Stage instructions for Costuming, Grouping, etc. 180 pages, paper covers.30 cts.
Bound in Boards, with cloth back..............................50 cts.

Kavanaugh's Humorous Dramas for School Exhibitions and Private Theatricals. Original and written expressly for School and Parlor performance. Paper.................................. 30 cts.
Boards..50 cts.

Dick's Diverting Dialogues. They are short, full of telling "situations," introducing easy dialect characters, and present the least possible difficulties in scenery and costume to render them exceedingly attractive. Paper...30 cts.
Boards..50 cts.

Dick's Comic Dialogues. Eight of the Dialogues are for males only, requiring from two to six characters; the remaining pieces are for both sexes. They are all bright, witty, very entertaining and full of droll and effective "situations." 184 pages, paper.......30 cts.
Bound in boards...50 cts.

Dick's Dialogues and Monologues. Containing entirely original Dialogues, Monologues, Farces, etc., etc., expressly designed for parlor performance, full of humor and telling "situations," and requiring the least possible preparation of Costumes and Scenery to make them thoroughly effective. 180 pages, paper............................30 cts.
Boards..50 cts.

Dick's Little Dialogues for Little People. Original and carefully selected Dialogues specially adapted for performance by young and quite young Children in Sunday School and other juvenile entertainments. Some of the Dialogues are exceedingly witty and effective; others are well suited for more serious occasions, and all of them entirely within the capabilities of small children.......................... 15 cts.

THEATRICALS, DIALOGUES AND CHARADES.

Burton's Amateur Actor. A complete Guide to Private Theatricals; giving plain directions for arranging, decorating and lighting the Stage; with rules and suggestions for mounting, rehearsing and performing all kinds of Plays, Parlor Pantomimes and Shadow Pantomimes. Illustrated with numerous engravings, and including a selection of original Plays, with Prologues, Epilogues, etc. Paper................**30 cts.**

Barmby's Musical Plays for Young People. These Plays are in Burlesque style and entirely in Rhyme; they are Comical in expression. Each Play includes the Vocal Score and Piano accompaniment to all Songs, Duets, and Choruses introduced. 201 pages, paper...**30 cts.**

Howard's Book of Drawing-Room Theatricals. A collection of twelve short and amusing plays. Some of the plays are adapted for performers of one sex only. 186 pages, paper..................**30 cts.**

Hudson's Private Theatricals. A collection of fourteen humorous plays. Four of these plays are adapted for performance by males only, and three are for females. 180 pages, paper...........**30 cts.**

Frost's Amateur Theatricals. A collection of eight original plays; all short, amusing and new. 180 pages, paper.............**30 cts.**

Parlor Theatricals; or, Winter Evenings' Entertainment. Containing Acting Proverbs, Dramatic Charades, Drawing-Room Pantomimes, a Musical Burlesque and an amusing Farce. Paper......**30 cts.**

Frost's Dramatic Proverbs and Charades. Containing eleven Proverbs and fifteen Charades, some for Dramatic Performance, and others arranged for Tableaux Vivants. 176 pages, paper..... **30 cts.**

Frost's Parlor Acting Charades. These twelve excellent and original Charades are arranged as short parlor Comedies and Farces, full of brilliant repartee and amusing situations. 182 pages, paper......**30 cts.**

Nugent's Burlesque and Musical Acting Charades. Containing ten Charades, all in different styles, two of which are easy and effective Comic Parlor Operas, with Music and Piano-forte Accompaniments. 176 pages, paper...**30 cts.**

McBride's Temperance Dialogues. Introducing Yankee, Dutch, Irish, Negro, and other dialect characters. 183 pages, paper.**30 cts.**

McBride's Humorous Dialogues. New Dialogues full of humor and witty repartee; some of them introducing Irish, Dutch, Yankee and other dialect characters. 192 pages, paper................**30 cts.**

McBride's Comic Dialogues. Twenty-three Original Humorous Dialogues, introducing a variety of comic Yankee characters, and other eccentricities. 180 pages, paper..........................**30 cts.**

McBride's New Dialogues. Containing Original Dialogues, introducing Irish, Yankee, and other eccentric characters. 16mo, 178 pages, paper...**30 cts.**

McBride's Funny Dialogues. New and Original Dialogues, introducing Yankee, Irish, Dutch, and other eccentric characters..**30 cts.**

*** **Any of the above may be had bound in boards. Price 50 cents.**

**WE WILL SEND A CATALOGUE free to any address, containing a list of all the Dialogues and Plays in each of the above books, together with the number of males and females required to perform them.*

POPULAR HAND-BOOKS.

Dick's Home Made Candies; or, How to Make Candy in the Kitchen. Containing complete Directions for making all the newest and most delicious Cream Confections, with boiled syrup, or by the French method without boiling: also the best receipts for all the favorite Candies, Bon-bons, Glaces, Caramels, Taffy, etc., with perfectly harmless flavorings and colorings, including all the information for syrup-boiling, clarifying, and the use of utensils, necessary to insure the most successful results..**25 cts.**

Confectioner's Hand-Book. Giving plain and practical directions for making Confectionery. Containing upward of three hundred Recipes, consisting of directions for making all sorts of Candies, Jellies, Comfits, Preserves, Sugar Boiling, Iced Liquors, Waters, Gum, Paste and Candy Ornaments, Syrups, Marmalades, Essences, Fruit, Pastes, Ice Creams, Icings, Meringues, Chocolates, etc., etc. A complete Hand-Book of the Confectioner's Art. Price.... ....**25 cts.**

The Amateur Trapper and Trap-Maker's Guide. A complete and carefully prepared treatise on the art of Trapping, Snaring and Netting. This comprehensive work is embellished with fifty engraved illustrations; and these, together with the clear explanations which accompany them, will enable anybody of moderate comprehension to make and set any of the traps described. It also gives the baits usually employed by the most successful Hunters and Trappers, and exposes their secret methods of attracting and catching animals, birds, etc., with scarcely a possibility of failure. Large 16mo, paper.............**50 cts.** Boards..**75 cts.**

Rarey & Knowlson's Complete Horse Tamer and Farrier. A New and Improved Edition, containing: Mr. Rarey's Whole Secret of Subduing and Breaking Vicious Horses; His improved plan of Managing Young Colts, and Breaking them to the Saddle, to Harness and the Sulky; Rules for Selecting a Good Horse, and for Feeding Horses. Also the Complete Farrier or Horse Doctor; being the result of fifty years' extensive practice of the author, John C. Knowlson, during his life an English Farrier of high popularity; containing the latest discoveries in the cure of Spavin. Illustrated with descriptive engravings. Boards, cloth..**50 cts.**

Holberton's Art of Angling; or, How and Where to Catch Fish. A practical Hand-Book for learners in everything that pertains to the art of fishing with Rod and Reel. By Wakeman Holberton, Fully Illustrated. It describes the special methods and appliances requisite to catch each variety of the finny tribe, and the most favorable localities to find them; with practical hints on camping out, necessary outfit, and the best choice of apparatus and baits, etc. Cloth, flexible...........**50 cts.**

The Amateur Printer; or, Type-Setting at Home. A thorough and complete instructor for the amateur in all the details of the Printer's Art, giving practical information in regard to type, ink, paper and all the implements requisite, with illustrated directions for using them in a proper manner. Paper...............................**25 cts.**

The Painter's Hand-Book. A thorough Guide to all that pertains to internal and external plain and tasteful House-painting. It explains the nature of the pigments or materials in general use, the best methods for their preparation and appliance, and the art of mixing colors to produce any desired tint or shade; with valuable receipts, hints and information to amateurs and experts......... ....**25 cts.**

BANJO AND BALL-ROOM GUIDES.

Dick's Quadrille Call-Book and Ball-Room Prompter.

Containing clear directions how to call out the figures of every dance, with the quantity of music necessary for each figure, and simple explanations of all the figures which occur in Plain and Fancy Quadrilles. This book gives plain and comprehensive instructions how to dance all the new and popular dances, fully describing

The Opening March or Polonaise,
Various Plain and Fancy Quadrilles,
Waltz and Glide Quadrilles,
Plain Lancers and Caledonians,
Glide Lancers and Caledonians,
Saratoga Lancers,
The Parisian Varieties,
The Prince Imperial Set,
Social and Basket Quadrilles,
Nine-Pin and Star Quadrilles,
Gavotte and Minuet Quadrilles,
March and Cheat Quadrilles,
Favorite Jigs and Contra-Dances,
Polka and Polka Redowa,
Redowa and Redowa Waltz,
Polka Mazourka and Old Style Waltz,
Modern Plain Waltz and Glide,
Boston Dip and Hop Waltz,
Five-Step Waltz and Schottische,
Varsovienne and Zulma L'Orientale,
Galop and Deux Temps,
Esmeralda, Sicilienne, Danish Dance,

AND OVER ONE HUNDRED FIGURES FOR THE "GERMAN";

To which is added a Sensible Guide to Etiquette and proper Deportment in the Ball and Assembly Room, besides seventy pages of dance music for the piano. Paper........ ....50 cts.
Bound in boards..75 cts.

Hillgrove's Ball-Room Guide and Complete Dancing-Master.

Containing a plain treatise on Etiquette and Deportment at Balls and Parties, with valuable hints on Dress and the Toilet, together with

Full Explanations of the Rudiments, Terms, Figures and Steps used in Dancing,
Including Clear and Precise Instructions how to dance all kinds of Quadrilles, Waltzes, Polkas, Redowas, Reels, Round, Plain and Fancy Dances, so that any person may learn them without the aid of a Teacher,
To which is added easy directions how to call out the Figures which belong

to every dance, and the amount of music required for each. Illustrated with 176 descriptive engravings. By T. Hillgrove, Professor of Dancing.
Bound in cloth, with gilt side and back..............................$1.00
Bound in boards..75 cts.

Frank Converse's Complete Banjo Instructor Without a Master.

Containing a choice collection of Banjo Solos and Hornpipes, Walk Arounds, Reels and Jigs, Songs and Banjo Stories, progressively arranged and plainly explained, enabling the learner to become a proficient banjoist without the aid of a teacher. The necessary explanations accompany each tune, and are placed under the notes on each page, plainly showing the string required, the finger to be used for stopping it, the manner of striking, and the number of times it must be sounded. The Instructor is illustrated with diagrams and explanatory symbols. Boards......50 cts.

The Banjo, and How to Play it.

Containing, in addition to the elementary studies, a choice collection of Polkas, Waltzes, Solos, Schottisches, Songs, Hornpipes, Jigs, Reels, etc., with full explanations of both the "Banjo" and "Guitar" styles of execution, and designed to impart a complete knowledge of the art of playing the Banjo practically, without the aid of a teacher. This work is arranged on the progressive system, showing the learner how to play the first few notes of a tune, then the next notes, and so on, a small portion at a time, until he has mastered the entire piece, every detail being as clearly and thoroughly explained as if he had a teacher at his elbow all the time. By Frank B. Converse, author of the "Banjo without a Master." 16mo, bound in boards, cloth back.50 cts.

GYMNASTICS, CALISTHENICS AND TRAINING.

Alexander's Calisthenics and Musical Drill for Little Children. Containing Fifty-nine Exercises, with numerous variations, introducing simple Calisthenics and Swimming Motions, Ring, Skipping and Marching Exercises, profusely illustrated, with Piano Music for every movement. A complete work on Recreative Calisthenics for young children and Primary School Classes. By A. Alexander, Professor of Calisthenics and Gymnastics. Paper..25 cts.

Cruden's Calisthenic Training and Musical Drill. A System of Physical Exercises as an aid to Teachers in Class Training. By George Cruden, A. M.
This work contains complete instructions in Military Marching, Dumb-Bell. and Indian Club Exercises; including Musical Drill in Free Gymnastics, Dumb-Bell and Bar-Bell Exercises and Hoop Drill, with explanatory illustrations and Piano Music for every movement. Boards.......50 cts.

Maclaren's Training in Theory and Practice. A Handbook of Training for all athletic exercises in accordance with the accepted modern theories and methods. It shows conclusively the errors and risks of the old styles of Training, and gives the most thorough ways of developing in the highest degree the muscular vigor, full respiration, and physical endurance which is indispensable to success in all athletic exercises and competitive exhibitions of strength, speed and skill. By Archibald Maclaren, Professor of Gymnastics of the Oxford University Gymnasium, England. Paper..50 cts.

Dick's Art of Gymnastics. Containing practical and progressive exercises applicable to all the principal apparatus of a well-appointed Gymnasium. Profusely illustrated. This work conveys plain and thorough instruction in the exercises and evolutions taught by the leading Professors of Gymnastics, so that proficiency may be attained, even without the aid of a Teacher. It also offers to Teachers a ready-arranged systematic course for their guidance. Cloth............$1.00.

Dick's Dumb-Bell and Indian Club Exercises. Containing practical and progressive instructions in the use of Dumb-Bells, Bar-Bells and Indian Clubs. Illustrated with cuts showing every position and motion of the body and limbs. Paper..........................25 cts.

The Laws of Athletics. How to Preserve and Improve Health, Strength and Beauty; and to Correct Personal Defects caused by Want of Physical Exercise. How to Train for Walking, Running, Rowing, etc., with the Systems of the Champion Athletes of the World. Including the Latest Laws of all Athletic Games and How to Play Them. By William Wood, Professor of Gymnastics. Paper...............25 cts.

Athletic Sports for Boys. Containing complete instructions in the manly accomplishments of Skating, Swimming, Rowing, Sailing, Horsemanship, Riding, Driving, Angling, Fencing and Broadsword. Illustrated with 194 wood-cuts. Boards..........................75 cts.

The Play-Ground ; or, Out-Door Games for Boys. A Book of Healthy Recreations for Youth, containing over a hundred Amusements, including Games of Activity and Speed, Games with Toys, Marbles, Tops, Hoops, Kites, Archery, Balls; with Cricket, Croquet and Base-Ball. Splendidly illustrated with 124 fine wood-cuts.
Boards..50 cts.

PHONOGRAPHY AND BOOK-KEEPING.

Pitman's Phonographic Teacher. A Practical Guide to Phonography or Phonetic Short-Hand. By Isaac Pitman. New edition revised and improved. This is acknowledged to be the best and most practical system of Short-Hand, and this work is the only original, thorough and reliable one of that system, which presents the fewest difficulties and the widest resources, entirely dispensing with the aid of a Teacher: and, although every system involves patience, perseverance and steady practice, Pitman's method ensures a more speedy acquisition of fluency and rapidity than any other......................15 cts.

Key to the Phonographic Teacher. An efficient aid to the learner in practicing and applying Pitman's Method of Short-hand, with exercises and explanations......................15 cts.

Pitman's Manual of Phonography. Containing a complete exposition of the system of Phonetic Short-hand, with numerous short-hand examples interspersed with the text, and exercises in reading. This Manual of Isaac Pitman's System, which is now being introduced as the Text-Book of Phonography in our educational institutions, has been revised and corrected, year after year, by its inventor, and is now presented in its latest and fullest perfection. Its pre-eminence is endorsed by the fact that its sales have already reached 650,000.
Convenient pocket size......................35 cts.

Key to the Exercises in Pitman's Manual. A great help for students......................15 cts.

Pitman's Phonographic Reporter; or, Reporter's Companion: An adaptation of Pitman's System to verbatim reporting. By Isaac Pitman. By the introduction of easily-acquired Phraseograms, Logograms, and other simple devices, time and labor are saved to such an extent that Reporters are enabled to keep pace with the most fluent speakers, and render accurate and verbatim reports, without elisions or condensation. This is the latest and crowning addition to the Phonographic art, and brings it up to the greatest practical perfection. Latest Edition, bound in boards......................50 cts.

The Young Reporter; or, how to Write Shorthand. Intended to afford thorough instructions to those who have not the assistance of an Oral Teacher. By the aid of this work, and the explanatory examples which are given as exercises, any person of ordinary intelligence may learn to write Shorthand, and report Speeches and Sermons in a short time. Boards......................50 cts.

Odell's System of Short-Hand. (Taylor Improved.) By which the method of taking down sermons, lectures, trials, speeches, etc., may be easily acquired, without the aid of a master. By this plan the difficulties of mastering this useful art are very much lessened, and the time required to attain proficiency reduced to the least possible limits...25 cts.

Day's Book-Keeping Without a Master. Containing the Rudiments of Book-keeping in Single and Double Entry, together with the proper Forms and Rules for opening and keeping condensed and general Book Accounts. This work is printed in a beautiful script type, and combines the advantages of a handsome style of writing with its very simple and easily understood lessons in Book-keeping. The several pages have explanations at the bottom, in small type, to assist the learner. As a pattern for opening book accounts it is especially valuable—particularly for those who are not well posted in the art......................50 cts.

Allyn's Ritual of Freemasonry. Containing a complete Key to the following Degrees: Degree of Entered Apprentice; Degree of Fellow Craft; Degree of Master Mason; Degree of Mark Master; Degree of Past Master; Degree of Excellent Master; Degree of Royal Arch; Royal Arch Chapter; Degree of Royal Master; Degree of Select Master; Degree of Super-Excellent Master; Degree of Ark and Dove; Degree of Knights of Constantinople; Degree of Secret Monitor; Degree of Heroine of Jericho; Degree of Knights of Three Kings; Mediterranean Pass; Order of Knights of the Red Cross; Order of Knights Templar and Knights of Malta; Knights of the Christian Mark, and Guards of the Conclave; Knights of the Holy Sepulchre; The Holy and Thrice Illustrious Order of the Cross; Secret Master; Perfect Master; Intimate Secretary; Provost and Judge; Intendant of the Buildings, or Master in Israel; Elected Knights of Nine; Elected Grand Master; Sublime Knights Elected; Grand Master Architect; Knights of the Ninth Arch; Grand Elect Perfect and Sublime Mason. Illustrated with 38 copper-plate engravings; to which is added, a Key to the Phi Beta Kappa, Orange, and Odd Fellows Societies. By Avery Allyn, K. R C. K. T. K. M., etc. 12mo, cloth..$5.00

Lester's "Look to the East." (Webb Work.) A Ritual of the First Three Degrees of Masonry. Containing the complete work of the Entered Apprentice, Fellow Craft, and Master Mason's Degrees, and their Ceremonies, Lectures, etc. Edited by Ralph P. Lester. This complete and beautiful Pocket Manual of the First Three Degrees of Masonry is printed in clear, legible type, and not obscured by any attempts at cypher or other perplexing contractions. It gives the correct routine of

Opening and Closing the Lodge in each Degree.
Calling off and Calling On.
Calling the Lodge Up and Down.
The Entire Ceremonies of Initiating Passing and Raising Candidates.
The Lectures all Ritually and Monitorially Complete.

Bound in cloth..$2.00
Leather tucks (pocket-book style) gilt edges........................2.50

Duncan's Masonic Ritual and Monitor; *or, Guide to the Three Symbolic Degrees of the Ancient York Rite, Entered Apprentice, Fellow Craft and Master Mason.* And to the Degrees of Mark Master, Past Master, Most excellent Master, and the Royal Arch. By Malcolm C. Duncan. Explained and Interpreted by copious Notes and numerous Engravings. This is a valuable book for the Fraternity, containing, as it does, the Modern "Work" of the order. No Mason should be without it.
Bound in cloth..$2.50
Leather tucks (pocket-book style) with gilt edges..................3.00

Duncan's Rituale der Freimaurerei. A Guide, in the German language, to the Three Symbolic Degrees of the Ancient York Rite. Dieses Werk ist geschrieben, um den jungern Mitglieder des Ordens einen Leitfaden an die Hand zu geben, und gibt eine genaue Beschreibung aller in der *Arbeit* gebräuchlichen Ceremonien, Zeichen, Worte, Griffe, u.s.w.
Leather tucks (pocket-book style), gilt edges.....................$2.00

Richardson's Monitor of Freemasonry. A complete Guide to the various Ceremonies and Routine in Freemasons' Lodges, Chapters, Encampments, Hierarchies, etc., in all the Degrees, whether Modern, Ancient, Ineffable, Philosophical or Historical. Containing, also, the Lectures, Addresses, Charges, Signs, Tokens, Grips, Passwords, Regalias and Jewels in each Degree. Profusely illustrated with Explanatory Engravings, Plans of the interior of Lodges, etc. Paper covers..........75 cts.
Bound in gilt..$1.25
Bound in leather tucks (pocket-book style).........................$2.00

BOOKS ON CARDS AND OTHER GAMES.

The American Hoyle; or, Gentleman's Hand-Book of Games. By "Trumps". This work has long since been accorded the position of an exclusive authority on games played in America. The FIFTEENTH EDITION, now issued, newly arranged, in new type, contains all the latest novelties, as well as the recent changes in games already in vogue, profusely illustrated. Among the new games introduced in this edition are Rubicon Piquet, Rubicon Bézique, Grabouche, Solo Whist, Cayenne Whist, Domino Whist, Cinch or High Five, Baccarat Banque and Baccarat Chemin de Fer, etc. In the game of Whist, the new features are "Cavendish's" rules for play, with best leads, and a critical examination of the system of "American Leads", elucidated by card illustrations; also, the mode of procedure in Duplicate Whist. The various games of Billiards and Pool, with the rules adopted in matches and tournaments, are inserted by permission of the Brunswick-Balke-Collender Company. The work also includes an exposition of the Doctrine of Chances.
Library Edition, 514 pages, 12 mo., cloth........................$1.50
A cheaper edition, 16 mo., in paper covers........................50 cts.
Bound in boards..75 cts.

Hoyle's Games. By "Trumps". A complete Manual of the games of skill and chance as played in America, and an acknowledged "arbiter on all disputed points"; thoroughly revised and corrected in accordance with the latest and best authorities. It contains the modern laws and complete instructions for the games of Chess, Draughts, Dominoes, Dice, Backgammon, and Billiards, as well as the games with cards at present in vogue, including Baccarat, Duplicate Whist, Cayenne Whist, Hearts, Grabouche, Newmarket, Solo Whist, Cinch or High Five, etc. Profusely illustrated. 16 mo, 514 pages, cloth........................$1 25
Bound in boards..75 cts.
Paper covers...50 cts.

"Trumps" New Card Games. Containing correct method and rules for playing the games of Hearts, Boodle, New Market, Five and Nine or Domino-Whist, Solo, and Cayenne Whist. Paper covers...25 cts.

Dick's Games of Patience; or Solitaire with Cards. New and Revised Edition. Containing Sixty-four Games. Illustrated with Fifty explanatory full-page Tableaux. This treatise on Solitaire embraces a number of new and original Games, and all the Games of Patience at present in favor with the most experienced players. Each game is carefully and lucidly described, with the distinctive rules to be observed and hints as to the best means of success in play. The Tableaux furnish efficient aid in rendering the disposition of the cards necessary to each game plain and easily comprehensible. The difficulty usually attending descriptions of intricate games is reduced, as far as possible, by precision in method and terseness of expression in the text, and the illustrations serve to dispel any possible ambiguity that might be unavoidable without their aid. Quarto, 143 pages, Board cover..............75 cts.
Cloth..$1.00

Parlor Tricks with Cards. Containing explanations of all the Tricks and Deceptions with playing Cards ever invented. The whole illustrated and made plain and easy with 70 engravings. Paper..30 cts.
Bound in boards, with cloth back...............................50 cts.

Dick's Art of Bowling; or, Bowler's Guide. Giving the correct method of playing, keeping the score, and the latest rules which govern the American and German Games, and their most popular variations; including the Regulations adopted in Matches and Tournaments.
Fully illustrated..25 cts.

ETIQUETTE AND PARLOR MAGIC.

Frost's American Etiquette; or, Laws of Good Society.

A condensed but thorough treatise on Etiquette and its Usages in America. Containing plain and reliable directions for correct deportment in every situation and under all circumstances in life, including special directions and instructions on the following subjects:—

Dinner Company and Invitations; Visiting, and Visiting Cards, Traveling, Riding and Driving; Balls, Morning and Evening Parties; Calls, Conversation and Street Etiquette; Salutes and Salutations; Weddings, Baptisms and Funerals; Church and Places of Amusement; Introductions and Letters of Introduction; Children, Hotel, and Card Table; Ladies' and Gentlemen's Toilet; Letter Writing and Servants.

BESIDES ONE HUNDRED UNCLASSIFIED LAWS APPLICABLE TO ALL OCCASIONS.

Paper covers...30 cts.
Bound in boards, cloth back...50 cts.

Martine's Hand-Book of Etiquette and Guide to True

Politeness. Containing clear and comprehensive directions for correct manners, conversation, dress, introductions, rules for good behavior at Dinner Parties and the Table, with the Etiquette of the Ball and Assembly Room, Evening Parties, and the usages to be observed when visiting or receiving calls; Deportment in the street and when traveling. To which is added the Etiquette of Courtship, Marriage, and fifty-six rules to be observed in general society. Bound in boards....................50 cts.
Bound in cloth, gilt sides..75 cts.

How to Shine in Society; or, The Science of Conversation.

Containing the principles, laws and general usages of polite society, including easily applied hints and directions for commencing and sustaining an agreeable conversation, and for choosing topics appropriate to the time, place and company, thus affording immense assistance to the bashful and diffident. 16mo. Paper covers..........................25 cts.

How to Behave; or, The Spirit of Etiquette. A Guide to

Polite Society, for Ladies and Gentlemen; containing rules for good behavior at the dinner table, in the parlor, and in the street; with important hints on introduction, conversation, etc.............................12 cts.

The Fireside Magician; or, The Art of Natural Magic

Made Easy. Being a scientific explanation of Legerdemain, Recreative Chemistry, Diversion with Cards, and of all the mysteries of Mechanical Magic, comprising two hundred and fifty interesting mental and physical recreations, with explanatory engravings. Paper.................30 cts.
Bound in boards, cloth back...50 cts.

The Parlor Magician; or, One Hundred Tricks for the

Drawing Room. Containing an extensive and miscellaneous collection of Conjuring, embracing: Tricks with Dice, Dominoes and Cards; Tricks with Ribbons, Rings and Fruit; Tricks with Coin, Handkerchiefs and Balls, etc. The whole illustrated with 121 engravings. Paper....30 cts.
Bound in boards with cloth back.....................................50 cts.

Morgan's Freemasonry Exposed and Explained. Showing

the Origin, History and Nature of Masonry, and containing a Key to all the Degrees of Freemasonry. Giving a clear and correct view of the manner of conferring the different degrees, as practiced in all Lodges..25 cts.

MINSTREL JOKES AND STUMP SPEECHES.

Dick's Stump Speeches and Minstrel Jokes. Containing Short and side-splitting Negro Acts and Farces, Eccentric Sketches, Stump Speeches, Darkey Lectures, End-Men's Jokes and Gags, Burlesque Sermons, Funny Dialogues, and everything necessary for a series of first-class Minstrel Entertainments; including the latest excruciations of modern Negro-Minstrelsy, and a number of startling originalities, risible rib-ticklers and hysterical button-starters. Paper....................30 cts.
Bound in boards, cloth back.......................................50 cts.

Dick's Ethiopian Scenes, Variety Sketches and Stump Speeches. Containing an inexhaustible collection of End-Men's Jokes.

Negro Interludes and Farces;
Fresh Dialogues for Interlocutor and Banjo;
New Stump Speeches;
Humorous Lectures;
Dialect Sketches and Eccentricities;
Dialogues and Repartee for Interlocutor and Bones;
Quaint Burlesque Sermons;
Jokes, Quips and Gags.

Paper covers...30 cts.
Bound in boards, cloth back.......................................50 cts.

Tambo's End-Men's Minstrel Gags. Containing some of the best jokes and repartees of the most celebrated "burnt cork" performers of our day. Tambo and Bones in all sorts and manner of scrapes. Also containing a rich collection of Darkey Dialogues, Sketches, Plantation Scenes, Eccentric Doings, Humorous Lectures, Laughable Interludes, Burlesque Stump Speeches, Mirth-provoking Witticisms, Conundrums, Yarns, Plantation Songs and Dances, etc., etc. Everything new and rich.
Paper covers...30 cts.
Bound in boards, cloth back.......................................50 cts.

Brudder Bones' Book of Stump Speeches and Burlesque Orations. Also containing Humorous Lectures, Ethiopian Dialogues, Plantation Scenes, Negro Farces and Burlesques, Laughable Interludes and Comic Recitations, interspersed with Dutch, Irish, French and Yankee Stories. This book contains some of the best hits and mirth-provoking jokes and repartees of the most celebrated End-Men of the day.
Paper covers. Price..30 cts.
Bound in boards, cloth back.......................................50 cts.

Howard's Book of Conundrums and Riddles. Containing over 1,200 of the best Conundrums, Riddles, Enigmas, Ingenious Catches and Amusing Sells ever invented. This splendid collection of curious paradoxes will afford the material for a never-ending feast of fun and amusement. Any person, with the assistance of this book, may take the lead in entertaining a company, and keep them in roars of laughter for hours together. Paper covers ....30 cts.
Bound in boards, cloth back ....50 cts.

Rowan's Riddles and Conundrums. A very choice gathering of Ancient, Modern, and quite recent Riddles and Conundrums, quaintly arranged, for amusement and merriment on opportune occasions. A first-rate pocket companion for Picnics and Winter Evenings.....15 cts.

Dick's Book of Alphabets. Containing a great variety of designs for plain and Fanciful Alphabets, Numerals and illuminated Initial letters in various colors, and elegant in style. It includes specimens of modern Ornamental designs, and of the ancient grotesque, Arabesque, and other eccentric devices for decoration and illumination, mainly gathered from rare old vellums and scarce books of past centuries. This work will be appreciated by Architects, Decorators, Designers, Draughtsmen, etc. Oblong quarto, full cloth...................................$1.50

GAMES AND AMUSEMENTS.

Dick's Parlor Exhibitions, and How to Make them Successful. Containing complete and detailed directions for preparing and arranging Parlor Exhibitions and Amateur Performances. It includes:

Tableaux Vivants.
Living Portraits.
Living Statuary.
Dame History's Peep Show.
Shadow Pantomimes.
Popular Ballads illustrated by appropriate action.
Charades of all kinds.
Parlor Pantomimes.
Punch and Judy.

AND FIFTY OTHER DIVERTING PARLOR PASTIMES AND AMUSEMENTS.

It contains also a full Catalogue of the Celebrated "ART EXHIBITION," and a practical treatise on the wonderful SCIENCE OF SECOND-SIGHT.

This work is thoroughly practical and gives the fullest instructions for preparing and lighting the stage, the construction of the FRAMES FOR LIVING PORTRAITS, and shows how each performance can be presented with complete success. It is illustrated with numerous engravings explaining the text. 150 pages, paper...**30 cts.**

Dick's One Hundred Amusements for Evening Parties, Picnics and Social Gatherings. This book is full of Original Novelties. It contains: New and Attractive Games, clearly illustrated by means of Witty Examples, showing how each may be most successfully played. Surpassing Tricks, easy of performance. Musical and other innocent sells. A variety of new and ingenious puzzles. Comical illusions, fully described. These surprising and grotesque illusions, are very startling in their effects, and present little or no difficulty in their preparation.

ALSO A NEW VERSION OF THE CELEBRATED "MRS. JARLEY'S WAX WORKS".

Illustrated by sixty fine wood engravings. Paper.... ....**30 cts.**

The Book of Fireside Games. Containing an explanation of a variety of Witty, Rollicking, Entertaining and Innocent Games and Amusing Forfeits, suited to the Family Circle as a Recreation. This book is just the thing for social gatherings, parties and picnics. Paper covers.**30 cts.**

The Book of 500 Curious Puzzles. A collection of Curious Puzzles and Paradoxes, Deceptions in Numbers, Amusing Tricks in Geometry; illustrated with a great variety of engravings. Paper..**30 cts.**

How to Amuse an Evening Party. A Complete collection of Home Recreations. Profusely Illustrated with over Two Hundred fine wood-cuts, containing Round Games and Forfeit Games, Parlor Magic and Curious Puzzles, Comic Diversions and Parlor Tricks, Scientific Recreations and Evening Amusements. Paper..........................**30 cts.**

Book of Riddles and 500 Home Amusements. Containing a curious collection of Riddles, Charades and Enigmas; Rebuses, Anagrams and Transpositions; Conundrums and Amusing Puzzles: Recreations in Arithmetic, and Queer Sleights, and numerous other Entertaining Amusements. Illustrated with 60 engravings. Paper............**30 cts.**

⁂ **Any of the above may be had bound in boards. Price 50 cts.**

The Secret Out; or 1,000 Tricks with Cards, and Other Recreations. Illustrated with over 300 engravings. A book which explains all the Tricks and Deceptions with Playing Cards ever known, and gives, besides, a great many new ones. The whole being described so carefully, with engravings to illustrate them, that anybody can easily learn how to perform them. This work also contains 240 of the best Tricks of Legerdemain, in addition to the Card Tricks. 400 pages, cloth....**$1.50**

DISTILLING AND MANUFACTURE OF LIQUORS.

Monzert's Practical Distiller. A complete Treatise on the Art of Distilling and Rectifying Alcohol, Liquors, Essences, Liqueurs, etc., by the latest and most improved methods. By Leonard Monzert. This work includes practical directions for Malting, Mashing, and Fermenting; Distilling, Rectifying and Purifying; it gives detailed instructions for constructing Stills, with all the connected appurtenances requisite for producing pure spirits, illustrated and explained by numerous diagrams. Also, all the necessary appliances for distilling Essences, Perfumes and Liqueurs, and for the best and most rapid method for the manufacture of Vinegar, including also the French Apparatus for continuous Distillation and Rectification combined in one process. It explains the principles of Alcoholmetry, with all the matter required for the guidance of the practical distiller, and for testing the quality and strength of resulting distillates, with correct Tables of comparative Percentages by weight and by volume, Degrees of Proof, and corresponding Specific Gravity. Bound in cloth, 12 mo.......... ....**$3.00**

The French Wine and Liquor Manufacturer. A Practical Guide and Receipt Book for the Liquor Merchant. Being a clear Treatise on the manufacture and Imitation of Brandy, Rum, Gin and Whiskey, with Practical Rules for the Manufacture and Management of all kinds of Wine, by Mixing, Boiling and Fermentation, as practiced in Europe; including instructions for Manufacturing Champagne Wine, and the most approved methods for making a variety of Cordials, Liquors, Punch Essences, Bitters and Syrups, together with a number of Recipes for Fining, Flavoring, Filtering and Coloring Wines and Liquors, for Restoring and Keeping Ale and Cider. Also containing the latest improvements for Manufacturing Vinegar by the Quick Method. To which is added Descriptive Articles on Alcohol, Distillation, Maceration and the use of the Hydrometer; with Tables, Comparative Scale, and 14 important Rules for Purchasing, Reducing and Raising the Strength of Alcohol, Etc. Illustrated by diagrams and engravings. Adapted for the Use and Information of the trade in the United States and Canada. By John Rack, Practical Liquor Manufacturer. Cloth.....................**$3.00**

Fleischman's Art of Blending and Compounding Liquors and Wines. Showing how all the leading and favorite Brands of Whiskeys, Brandies and other Liquors and Wines are prepared for the trade by Rectifiers, etc., at the present time; with complete and correct receipts for making all the ingredients, flavoring, &c., employed in their manufacture, and the actual cost of each product as offered for sale. By Joseph Fleischman. By the aid of this ENTIRELY NEW WORK, Liquor Dealers and Saloon keepers can easily prepare as good liquors as they can buy, or better, at a large saving in outlay, This thoroughly practical work also affords all the necessary information relating to Whiskeys in Bond; it gives the distillery values when first bonded, the loss in bulk and increase in proof at the end of each six months, the method by which the duty is calculated, and the values when finally withdrawn from bond, duty paid. It also contains valuable and recent receipts for preparing the finest qualities of Liquors, Cordials, Bitters, &c., and everything in it is NEW, RELIABLE AND THOROUGH. 12mo, cloth.........**$2.00**

Lacour on the Manufacture of Liquors, Wines and Cordials, Without the aid of Distillation. Also, the Manufacture of Effervescing Beverages and Syrups, Vinegar and Bitters. Prepared and arranged expressly for the Trade. By Pierre Lacour. By the use of this book every man can make all kinds of liquors, wines, cordials, vinegar and syrups at home, without the use of any apparatus of any kind. The work is by the French chemist, Lacour, of Bordeaux. Cloth................**$2.50**

BOOKS ON CARD GAMES.

Blackbridge's Complete Poker Player. A Practical Guide-Book to the American National Game; containing mathematical and experimental analyses of the probabilities of Draw Poker. By JOHN BLACKBRIDGE, Actuary. This, as its title implies, is an exhaustive treatise on Draw Poker, giving minute and detailed information on the various chances, expectations, possibilities and probabilities that can occur in all stages of the game, with directions and advice for successful play, deduced from actual practice and experience, and founded on precise mathematical data. Small quarto, 142 pages, paper....................50 cts.
Bound, cloth..$1.00

Proctor on Draw-Poker. By Prof. RICHARD A. PROCTOR. An interesting Treatise on the Laws and Usages which govern the Game of Draw-Poker, with Practical Remarks upon the Chances and Probabilities of the Game, and a Critical Analysis of the Theories and Statistics advanced by Blackbridge and other writers, and especially in regard to their doctrines relating to cumulative recurrences..........................15 cts.

Talk of Uncle George to his Nephew About Draw Poker. Containing valuable suggestions in connection with this Great American Game; also instructions and directions to Clubs and Social Card Parties. Illustrated. Paper...25 cts.

How Gamblers Win; or, The Secrets of Advantage Playing Exposed. Being a complete and scientific exposé of the manner of playing all the numerous advantages in the various Card Games, as practised by professional gamblers. This work is designed as a warning to self-confident card-players. Boards..............................50 cts.

The Thompson Street Poker Club. A true and authentic record of the astonishing poker play perpetrated by this notorious "Culled" Club with their peculiar hands, and summarily simple mode of settlements, portraying the peculiar humor, oddities and extravagances of the Negro in his happiest vein. Profusely illustrated by E. W. Kemble, in his most mirth-provoking style........................25 cts.

The Mott Street Poker Club. Being the Secretary's Minutes of each session of this celebrated Chinese Club from its foundation to its close; a full revelation of its proceedings, and the ludicrous incidents arising from the eccentric ways of playing adopted by the guileless members of the club, and the astounding poker hands held by the tricky "Heathen Chinee." Profusely illustrated by Michal Woolf..25 cts.

Draw-Poker for Poker Players. A Condensed Treatise on the Game, explaining the Technical Terms used, the relative value of the Hands, and complete directions for successful play, including Schenck's Rules. Vest pocket size, illustrated...............................15 cts.

American Whist. Containing a full description of the Game, Technical Terms, Rules for successful Play, the Laws of the Game, and a specimen Game with the Hands played throughout. Vest pocket size, fully illustrated...15 cts.

Day's Fortune-Telling Cards. We have just printed an original set of cards for telling fortunes, which are an improvement on any hitherto made. They are so arranged that each answer will respond to every one of the questions which may be put. These cards will also afford a fund of amusement in a party of young people. Each pack is enclosed in a card case, on which are printed directions..........30 cts.

LOVE, COURTSHIP AND MATRIMONY.

The Art and Etiquette of Making Love. A Manual of Love, Courtship and Matrimony. It tells

How to cure bashfulness,
How to commence a courtship,
How to please a sweetheart or lover,
How to write a love-letter,
How to "pop the question",
How to act before and after a proposal,
How to accept or reject a proposal,
How to break off an engagement,
How to act after an engagement,
How to act as bridesmaid or groomsman,
How the etiquette of a wedding and all the details of the after reception should be observed,

And in fact, how to fulfill every duty and meet every contingency connected with courtship and matrimony. 176 pages. Paper covers.. **30 cts.** Bound in boards, cloth back................................**50 cts.**

Howard's Book of Love Poetry. A curious and Beautiful Collection of Tenderly Delicate, Sweetly Pathetic and Amusingly Quizzical Poetical Love-Addresses, containing a large number of the most admired selections from the leading Poets suitable for quotations in Love Letters, and applicable to all phases and contingencies incident to the tender passion. 141 pages................................**25 cts.**

Courtship Made Easy; or, The Art of Making Love Fully Explained. Containing full directions for Conducting a Courtship with Ladies of every age and Position in society, and valuable information for persons who desire to enter the marriage state. Also, forms of Love-letters to be used on certain occasions. 64 pages..................**15 cts.**

How to Win and How to Woo. Containing Rules for the Etiquette of Courtship, showing how to win the favor of the Ladies, how to begin and end a Courtship, and how to write Love-Letters......**15 cts.**

The Language of Flowers. A complete dictionary of the Language of Flowers, and the sentiments which they express. Well arranged and comprehensive in every detail. All unnecessary matter has been omitted. This little volume is destined to fill a want long felt for a reliable book at a price within the reach of all. Paper..........**15 cts.**

Dictionary of Love. Containing a Definition of all the terms used in the History of the Tender Passion, together with specimens of curious model love letters, and many other interesting matters appertaining to Love, never before published; the whole forming a remarkable Text-Book for all Lovers, as well as a Complete Guide to Matrimony, and a Companion of Married Life. Paper................................**50 cts.**

Anecdotes of Love. Being a true account of the most remarkable events connected with the History of Love in all ages and among all Nations. By LOLA MONTEZ, Countess of Landsfeldt. Paper..**50 cts.**

Poet's Companion. A Dictionary of all Allowable Rhymes in the English Language. This gives the Perfect, the imperfect and Allowable Rhymes, and will enable you to ascertain to a certainty whether any word can be mated. It is invaluable to any one who desires to court the Muses, and is used by some of the best writers in the country....**25 cts.**

Green's 100 Tricks With Cards, BY J. H. GREEN, reformed Gambler. This is a book of 96 pages, and exposes and explains all the mysteries of the Gambling Table. It is interesting not only to those who play, but to those who do not. Old Players will get some new ideas from this curious book. Paper................................**30 cts.**

The Wizard of the North's Hand-Book of Natural Magic. Being a series of Tricks of Deception, arranged for Amateurs. By Professor J. H. ANDERSON. Paper................................**25 cts.**

Madame Le Normand's Fortune Teller. A party of ladies and gentlemen may amuse themselves for hours with this curious book. It tells fortunes by "The Chart of Fate" (a large lithograpic chart), and gives 624 answers to questions on every imaginable subject that may happen in the future. It explains a variety of ways for telling fortunes by Cards and Dice; gives a list of 79 curious old superstitions and omens, and 187 weather omens, and winds up with the celebrated Oraculum of Napoleon. Boards.. 40 cts.

Le Normand's Fortune Telling Cards. These cards are the Oracle of Destiny by which Mlle. Le Normand of Paris, the most wonderful Fortune Teller that ever existed, was enabled to establish a reputation for over one hundred years extending all over the world. By their aid the possibility is offered to all of reading their own destiny as well as that of others. They foreshadow good and bad fortunes, fidelity and falsehood, happiness and misery, safety and peril, peace and strife, matrimony, life and death. Thirty-six cards handsomely printed in colors with English and German explanations. All in a neat box........50 cts.

Fontaine's Golden Wheel Dream-Book and Fortune Teller, containing an alphabetical list of Dreams, with their interpretation and the lucky numbers they signify. It explains how to tell Fortunes with Cards, Dice, Dominoes, Coffee Grounds, etc., and the Golden Wheel, of which a large Colored Lithographic Engraving is folded and bound in with the book. It shows how to foretell future events by the Lines on the hand, by Moles on the body, by the Face, Finger-nails, Hair and Shape of the Head, and gives lucky and unlucky days. Boards........ 40 cts.

Pettengill's Perfect Fortune Teller and Dream-Book. It is compiled with great care from authorities on Astrology, Geology, Chiromancy, Necromancy, Spiritual Philosophy, etc., etc. Among the subjects treated of, are: Casting Nativities by the Stars, Telling Fortunes by Lines on the Hand, by Moles on the Body, by Turning Cards, by Questions of Destiny, by Physical Appearances, by the Day of Birth, etc. A book of 144 pages. Boards..40 cts.

Le Marchand's Fortune Teller and Dreamer's Dictionary. Containing a complete Dictionary of Dreams, with a clear interpretation of each Dream. Also showing how to tell fortunes by the Lady's Love Oracle. How to foretell the Sex of Children. How to tell any Person's Age. To know who your future Husband will be, and how soon you will be Married. How to tell Future events with Cards, Dice, Tea and Coffee Grounds, Eggs, Apple Parings and the Lines of the Hand.
144 pages. Boards..40 cts.

The Egyptian Dream-Book and Fortune Teller. Containing an Alphabetical list of dreams, with their signification and their lucky numbers. Illustrated with explanatory diagrams. Boards......40 cts.

The Independent Liquorist; or, The Art of Manufacturing all kinds of Syrups, Bitters, Cordials, Champagnes, Wines, Lager Beer, Ale, Porter, Beer, Punches, Tinctures, Extracts, Brandy, Gin, Essences, Flavorings, Colorings, Sauces, Catsups, Pickles, Preserves, etc. By L. Monzert, Practical Liquorist and Chemist. Every Druggist, Grocer, Restaurant, Hotel-keeper, Farmer, Fruit Dealer, Wine Merchant, should have a copy of this work. 12mo, cloth $3.00

The Bordeaux Wine and Liquor Dealer's Guide. A Treatise on the Manufacture of French Wines and Liquors, with full directions to the Liquor Dealer how to manage his Liquors, Wines, etc., etc. A book of great value to every person who deals in Foreign and American Spirituous Liquors, or Foreign Wines, Cordials, etc. 12mo, cloth........$2.50

FORTUNE TELLERS AND DREAM BOOKS.

The Gipsy Witches Dream Book and Fortune Teller. Containing a complete list of Dreams with their significations; the art of foretelling future events by Cards, Dice, Dominoes, Tea and Coffee grounds, etc. This comprehensive book also gives complete directions for reading individual character by the form, hair and features; also a full explanation of signs and auguries, the signification of moles as they occur on various parts of the body, and a full list of lucky days, weeks, months, etc..25 cts.

Mother Shipton's Fortune-Teller; or Future Fate Foretold by the Planets. Being the 900 Answers of Pythagoras to the Questions of Life's Destiny. Derived from the Mystic Numbers and Letters of the Planets. Containing the Emblematical and Mystical Wheel of Fortune and Fate, colored. 115 pages, paper...... .....30 cts.

Mother Shipton's Oriental Dream Book. Being a reliable interpretation of Dreams, Visions, Apparitions, etc. Together with a History of Remarkable Dreams, proven true as interpreted. Collected and arranged from the most celebrated masters. Paper..........30 cts.

The Everlasting Fortune-Teller and Magnetic Dream-Book. Containing the Science of Foretelling Events by the Signs of the Zodiac; Lists of Lucky and Unlucky Days; List of Fortunate Hours; the Science of Foretelling Events by Cards, Dice, Dominoes, etc; the Science of Foretelling anything in the Future by Dreams; and also containing NAPOLEON'S ORACULUM; or, The Book of Fate.............30 cts.

Mother Carey's Dream-Book and Fortune-Teller. Containing the method of Fortune-Telling with Cards; a complete Dreamer's Dictionary; the Science of Palmistry, or telling Fortunes by the Lines of the Hand; how to tell a Person's Character by a list of Lucky and Unlucky days and hours; how to tell with Cards which of Three Ladies has the best Husband. Mathematical Tables for telling any Person's Age.................. ....15 cts.

Aristotle's Book of Fate and Dictionary of Dreams. Containing Dreams and their Interpretations; the Signification of Moles on Men and Women; one hundred and eighty-seven Weather Omens; Hymen's Lottery and Aristotie's Oraculum or Book of Fate..........15 cts.

The Hindoo Fortune-Teller and Oracle of Destiny. Containing Ten Methods of Telling Fortunes with Cards, a complete system of Fortune Telling with Dice, together with Sixty-seven Good and Bad Omens, with their interpretation......... ....15 cts.

The Combination Fortune-Teller and Dictionary of Dreams. A comprehensive Encyclopedia explaining all the different methods extant by which good and evil events are foretold, containing 430 pages and illustrated with numerous engravings and two large colored lithographs. 16mo, cloth.................................$1.25

The Ladies' Love Oracle; or, Counselor to the Fair Sex. A Complete Fortune-Teller and Interpreter of all questions upon Love, Courtship and Marriage..30 cts.

Napoleon's Oraculum and Book of Fate. Containing the famous Papers found in the Cabinet of Napoleon Bonaparte, and a full exposition of Chiromancy or Palmistry.........................10 cts.

Chilton's One Thousand Secrets and Wrinkles. Containing 1,000 useful hints and receipts. No family should be without this little storehouse of valuable information. Paper......................30 cts.

BOXING AND WRESTLING.

How to Join a Circus. This contains all the information necessary for those who desire to qualify themselves for the Circus or Gymnasium; with hints to Amateurs and advice to Professional performers; affording thorough instruction in all branches of the business. Illustrated. By the celebrated Tony Denier. By carefully following the advice and instruction contained in this book, any person with a moderate degree of perseverance can become proficient in all the startling acts on the horizontal bar, flying trapeze, and other evolutions that challenge the admiration of all who behold them. 104 pages..............25 cts.

Jerry Thomas' Bar Tender's Guide; or How to Mix all kinds of Fancy Drinks. *An entirely new edition; new plates; new drinks.* Containing clear and reliable directions for mixing all the beverages used in the United States. Embracing Punches, Juleps, Cobblers, Cocktails, etc., etc., in endless variety. By Jerry Thomas. This work also contains the best receipts for preparing bottled Punch, bottled Cocktails, Punch Essences, etc., after the most approved methods; also, all the newest Egg Noggs, Fizzes, Slings, Sours, and other Fancy Drinks in endless variety. 16mo, illuminated paper cover..........................50 cts.
16mo, cloth..75 cts.

Dick's Art of Wrestling. A New Hand-Book of thorough instruction in Wrestling, with the accepted Rules to be observed in the different methods of wrestling generally adopted at the present time. Fully illustrated by well-designed engravings, exhibiting all the aggressive and defensive positions necessary for success................25 cts.

Price's Science of Self-Defense. Illustrated with Engravings. This book was written by Ned Price, the celebrated boxer, and is the best work that was ever written upon the subject of Sparring and Wrestling. It contains all the tricks and stratagems resorted to by professional boxers, and the descriptions of the passes, blows and parries are all clearly explained by the aid of numerous diagrams and engravings. That portion of the work which treats on wrestling is particularly thorough, and is well illustrated with engravings. Boards..........................75 cts.

Ned Donnelly's Art of Boxing. A thorough Manual of Sparring and Self-Defence, illustrated with Forty Engravings, showing the various Blows, Stops and Guards; by Ned Donnelly, Professor of Boxing to the London Athletic Club, etc., etc. This work explains in detail every movement of attack and defence in the clearest language, and in accordance with the most approved and modern methods; the engravings are very distinctly drawn, and show each position and motion as plainly as the personal instruction of a professor could convey it. It teaches all the feints and dodges practised by experienced boxers, and gives advice to those who desire to perfect themselves in the Manly Art. Including the London Prize Ring Rules, and revised Marquis of Queensbury's Rules. 127 pages..25 cts.

The Art of Attack and Defence. A Manual of Fencing, Sword Exercise, Bayonet Practice and Boxing, affording instructions in the modern method of Fencing, the mode of attack with sword against sword or bayonet, and with bayonet against sword or bayonet. By Major W. J. Elliott. Profusely illustrated......................................25 cts.

Boxing Made Easy; or, The Complete Manual of Self-Defense. Clearly explained and Illustrated in a Series of Easy Lessons, with some important Hints to Wrestlers...............................15 cts.

COOK BOOKS.

Dinner Napkins, and How to Fold Them. Containing plain and systematic directions for arranging and folding Napkins or Serviettes for the Dinner Table, from the simplest forms to the most elaborate and artistic designs. By Georgiana C. Clark. This little work embraces all the favorite designs in general use for transforming a plain Napkin into one of the most attractive and ornamental appendages to an elegantly arranged Dinner-Table. Some of the patterns being expressly intended for combining artistic display with floral decoration, appropriately symbolic of Bridal and other special occasions.
Profusely illustrated..**25 cts.**

Mrs. Crowen's American Lady's Cookery Book. Giving every variety of information for ordinary and holiday occasions, and containing over 1,200 Original Receipts for Preparing and Cooking Soups and Broths, Fish and Oysters, Clams, Mussels, Crabs and Terrapins, Meats of all kinds, Poultry and Game, Eggs and Cheese, Vegetables and Salads, Sauces of all kinds, fancy Desserts, Puddings and Custards, Pies and Tarts, Bread and Biscuit, Rolls and Cakes, Preserves and Jellies, Pickles and Catsups, Potted Meats, etc., etc. The whole being a complete system of American Cookery. By Mrs. T. J. Crowen.
480 pages, 12 mo., cloth..**$1.50**

How to Cook and How to Carve. Giving plain and easily understood directions for preparing and cooking, with the greatest economy, every kind of dish, with complete instructions for serving the same. This Book is just the thing for a young Housekeeper. It is worth a dozen of expensive French books. Paper covers................**30 cts.**
Bound in boards with cloth back..**50 cts.**

The American Home Cook Book. Containing several hundred excellent recipes. The whole based on many years' experience of an American Housewife. Illustrated with engravings. All the recipes in this book are written from actual experience in Cooking. Paper...**30 cts.**
Boards..**50 cts.**

The Yankee Cook Book. A new system of Cookery. Containing hundreds of excellent recipes from actual experience in Cooking; also, full explanation in the art of Carving. 126 pages, paper covers.**30 cts.**
Boards..**50 cts.**

Soyer's Standard Cookery for the People. Embracing an entirely new System of Plain Cookery and Domestic Economy. By Alexis Soyer. The plain and familiar style adopted in describing the details of the various culinary operations, commends itself to the notice of all economical housekeepers, as it affords the best results with the least expenditure. 214 pages, paper..**30 cts.**
Boards..**50 cts.**

The American Housewife and Kitchen Directory. This valuable book embraces three hundred and seventy-eight recipes for cooking all sorts of American dishes in the most economical manner.
Paper..**30 cts.**
Boards..**50 cts.**

Souillard's Book of Practical Receipts. For the use of Families, Druggists, Perfumers. Confectioners and Dealers in Soaps and Fancy Articles for the Toilet. By F. A. Souillard. Paper......... **25 cts.**

Book of Wonders, Mysteries and Disclosures. A complete hand-book of useful information. Giving a large number of Recipes for the manufacture of valuable articles of every-day use, and of great value to manufacturers, storekeepers, druggists, peddlers and families. To which is added Taxidermy and Traps and Trapping. Paper......**25 cts.**

The Perfect Gentleman. A book of Etiquette and Eloquence. Containing information and instruction for those who desire to become brilliant or conspicuous in General Society, or at Parties, Dinners or Popular Gatherings, etc. It gives directions how to use wine at table, with Rules for judging the quality thereof, Rules for Carving, and a complete Etiquette of the Dinner Table, including Dinner Speeches, Toasts and Sentiments, Wit and Conversation at Table, etc. It has also an American Code of Etiquette and Politeness for all occasions. It also contains all the necessary information relating to the rules of Etiquette to be observed in fashionable and official society at Washington, and this alone makes it valuable to any one who visits that city, either for pleasure or business. It also contains, Model Speeches, with directions how to deliver them, Duties of the Chairman at Public Meetings, Forms of Preambles and Resolutions, etc. It is a handsomely bound volume of 335 pages. **$1.50**

The American Boy's Own Book of Sports and Games. A work expressly designed to amuse and instruct American Boys at all times and seasons, both in and out doors. This work contains 600 pages, and is illustrated with over 600 engravings and diagrams, drawn by White and other American and English artists, and engraved by N. Orr, in his best style. It is also embellished with eight full-page ornamental titles, executed in the highest style of art, on tinted paper, illustrating the different departments of the work. An elegant gift for a boy, affording endless amusement, instruction and recreation.
12 mo., extra fine cloth, gilt side and back stamp.................. **$2.00**

The Twelve Decisive Battles of the War. A History of Eastern and Western Campaigns in relation to the Battles which decided their issue, and their important bearings on the result of the Struggle for the Union. By William Swinton. Illustrated by seven steel portraits of the leading Generals and nine maps of battle-fields. This work is the result of the author's personal experiences, and based on the records of the Generals commanding on both sides; it is, therefore, thorough, impartial and reliable. 520 pages. 8vo. Extra cloth, beveled, **$3.50**

Day's Cards of Courtship. Arranged with such apt conversations, that you will be enabled to ask the momentous question categorically, in such a delicate manner that the young lady will not suspect what you are at. These cards may be used either by two persons, or they will make lots of fun for an evening party of young people. When used in a party, the question is read aloud by the lady receiving it—she shuffles and hands out an answer—and that also must be read aloud by the gentleman receiving it. The fun thus caused is intense. Put up in handsome cases, on which are printed directions.................................. **30 cts.**

Day's Love-Letter Cards· or, Love-Making Made Easy. We have just printed a novel set of Cards which will delight the hearts of young people susceptible of the tender passion. Both letters and answers are either humorous or humorously sentimental—thus creating lots of fun when used at a party of young people—and special pains has been taken with them to avoid that silly, sentimental formality so common in printed letters of this kind. Put up in handsome cases, on which are printed directions.................. ....**30 cts.**

Day's Conversation Cards. A New and Original Set, comprising Eighteen Questions and Twenty-four Answers, so arranged that the whole of the answers are apt replies to each one of the eighteen questions. The plan of these cards is very simple, and easily understood. Used by a party of young people, they will make a good deal of fun. The set comprises forty-two Cards in the aggregate, which are put up in a handsome case, with printed directions for use.......................**30 cts.**

www.ingramcontent.com/pod-product-compliance
Lightning Source LLC
Chambersburg PA
CBHW030541270326
41927CB00008B/1467

* 9 7 8 3 3 3 7 3 1 4 4 6 0 *